THE FACE OF SOUTH VIETNAM

THE FACE OF SOUTH VIETNAM

text by Dean Brelis

photographs by Jill Krementz

Houghton Mifflin Company   Boston   1968

First Printing   w

CONTENTS

Part I

Part II

17 TH PARALLEL

Quang Tri
HUE

LAOS

Da Nang
Hoi An
Tam Ky

THAILAND

Quang
Ngai

Central
Vietnam
Lowlands

Kon Tum

Bong Son

Central
Vietnam
Highlands

Qui Nhon

Plei Ku

Song Cau

CAMBODIA

Hau Bon

Tuy Hoa

Ban Me Thuot

Nha
Trang

SOUTH

South Vietnam East

Gia Nghia

Da Lat

Phuoc Bin

CHINA

An Loc

Bao Loc

Di
Linh

Phan
Rang

Tay Ninh

Phuoc
Vinh

SEA

Phu
Cuong
Bien
Hoa

Xuan
Loc

Phan Thiet

Chau
Doc
Cao
Lanh
Moc Hoa

Hau
Nghia

SAIGON

Ham
Tan

Ha Tien

Long
Xuyen
Sadec

Tan An

Go Cong

Phuoc
Le

My Tho

REPUBLIC

Vinh Long
Truc
Giang

Vung Tau

Duong
Dong
Rach Gia

Can
Tho

Phu Vinh

of VIETNAM

Vi
Thanh

Khanh
Hung

South
Vietnam
West

Bac Lieu

NATIONAL BOUNDARIES

Quang Long
(Ca Mau)

PROVINCE BOUNDARIES

Con Son

0   25   50   100

MILES

THE FACE OF SOUTH VIETNAM

PART I

text by Dean Brelis

My part of this book is for
Anne and Phil, Dorothy and Ivan.

D.B.

1. TWENTY YEARS OF AGONY

It was a four-engined DC–6, and it looked old and forced because the yellow and orange colors on the tail and the face of a fire-breathing dragon near the door were gaudy, as if to hide the age. We had been told that it would be a Caravelle; but at the last moment, the one and only Caravelle in the Air Vietnam stable had been taken over by Prime Minister Nguyen Cao Ky, who was going off on a holiday to Hong Kong and Formosa. The Vietnamese air hostess spoke English with a French accent. In her blue and white uniform, with her white gloves, she was pretty and polite. We took off from Bangkok toward Saigon.

*

Now, in the plane, looking through the round window and seeing beyond the fleecy rags of clouds, the ground far below, a land that looked unconcerned and green, I wondered if we had reached Vietnam yet, or whether it was Cambodia. The air hostess' voice broke through my reverie, saying in Vietnamese first, and then French, finally English, that we were landing at Phnom Penh. The plane was filled with a horde of French-speaking tourists, and they were fat and all carried cameras. They also had maps and pamphlets to fortify them for a visit to Angkor Wat, one of the great havens of an archaeological past, a dead city, a ruin that touches deeply back into a thousand-year-old past when the land below was warring for its identity, even as I knew it still was. I realized how petty time is in this regard, and how little is revealed to one generation after another, of the mistakes that have been made, and what should have been learned.

The Americans were alone in the plane now. We couldn't disembark because we were Americans and we were not welcome. The delicacy of memory was suddenly sharp in my mind. I knew that Americans had parachuted into Vietnam during World War II and worked with Ho Chi Minh. I knew something about the events that had followed: the revolutionary phrases that had rung out through North and South Vietnam, the French challenged as the colonial god ruler, the people of Vietnam quoting from our Declaration of Independence that all men are created equal. The play and the tragedy of that time came back to me as we waited in a too hot airplane, standing on the ground, and the hostility against the American like an invisible curtain, as thick, as unsettling and sticky as the ground mist that had a distasteful sense of everything wrong.

The Allied actions in North and South Vietnam had opened the floodtide of hate we were still feeling, twenty years later, in the summer of 1965, when Americans by the tens of thousands were arriving in Vietnam. They had come to fight a war, one that had begun in 1945, when Ho Chi Minh and his people had proclaimed themselves free from the French.

During the Second World War Ho Chi Minh had identified himself with the Allies in word as well as in deed. After V-J Day the British and the Chinese were sent into Vietnam to establish law and order. The country was divided in half, at the sixteenth parallel, with the British taking the southern half, and the Chinese moving into the northern half. The idea that the Vietnamese had any right to self-determination was well beyond the British. They wholly misunderstood the meaning of the government established by the people of Vietnam — the English identified with the past sense of law and order, meaning the French colonialism that had destroyed some 20,000 schools the Vietnamese had created in their country before the French came in 1858; by the time the Second World War arrived to engulf Southeast Asia and the people of Vietnam, the French permitted only 144 secondary schools throughout all of Vietnam. Perhaps the British of 1945 felt that by reestablishing the French in Vietnam, they would also enhance their own position with regard to India. But British presence in Vietnam, in the fatefull fall of 1945, only intercepted history. It did not stop it. The British were incapable of imagining Ho's government set up in Saigon's Hotel de Ville as legitimate. They wanted the tricolor of France raised over Vietnam, and to make certain this would happen they rallied around the Indian forces at their disposal a large group of the Japanese whose surrender they had come to accept, and put those Japanese at work to rearm the French and destroy the government the people of Vietnam had established — a government that included all the people of Vietnam, North and South. When the British movements in the South became apparent, there were widespread demonstrations by Vietnamese people, and the result was the first of countless days when blood ran in the streets of Saigon.

The sound of gunfire and the desolate agony of human collision and blood was still the sight and smell of Saigon in 1965. Ho Chi Minh was no longer in Saigon. But he was in Hanoi, and if his government did not prevail throughout Vietnam, it existed, in North Vietnam. And now, Viet Cong forces loyal to the idea that South Vietnam should be a Communist nation, were about to finish off Saigon. In the spring and summer of 1965, America entered the twenty-year-old conflict, out of fear that a Communist government in South Vietnam would mean the collapse of all Southeast Asia. There had been many foreign powers "doctoring" to what they felt were the ills of Vietnam. The Americans were not the first, but it appeared they would be the last. Apart from some token support from a few countries, the United States was to stand alone in Vietnam.

❋

I had really decided that I would go back to Vietnam in the spring of 1965 when I had seen a copy of *Life* magazine and the superb picture essay by Larry Burrows of the Marine dying in a helicopter mission over Vietnam. The pictures, all in black and white from the cover on through the end where one of the survivors of the mission breaks down and cries, imparted a feeling of catastrophe and courage. The *Life* story showed all that is noble in the individual, and yet at the same time, it had an overpowering furious message for me. I worked and reported throughout the Middle East and parts of Africa, the dysentery beat as I called it in my lighter moments; the message I found in the Burrows story was that away from Vietnam I was removed from myself. I was on the outside in those countries in the sense that I wasn't roused by the unexpected. I didn't try to analyze the events I reported and expect them to have a direct relationship to me. But Larry Burrows' picture essay remained with me, ever present, and I had the impression that what was happening in Vietnam was something I couldn't remain detached from. I felt that the suffering of Vietnam was chilling, and to the extent that I was an American and that I had seen and suffered through some of my country's earlier wounds, I had to go to Vietnam where pain was close to my own people. There was nothing capricious in my heart or mind as we sat in Phnom Penh waiting for the takeoff to Saigon. I kept thinking about the stories I had heard about Viet Cong coming up to you in the street and sticking a needle into your arm, the point poisoned, and when that passed out of my mind there were visions of kidnappings, and after that the well-known scene in anyone's mind who has paid attention to Vietnam, the flash of a downtown bombing and women holding their bleeding faces. The reputation of Saigon, even when one takes into account the normal exaggeration of sensational news reports, was comparable to that of Central Park after dark, when anything can happen if you walk through the darker places alone.

We landed at Saigon early in the evening. It was dark and raining, and my first impression was that I had never been there before, even though I had landed in Saigon in 1950. The entire airfield was overgrown with a wide assortment of military aircraft, all with U.S. Air Force markings. The giant CN–130's, the Hercules, as they are called, so clean-looking and shiny and with such an air of influence about them that they seemed to have no business with war; the helicopters that were everywhere, as if their departures and arrivals were part of the beat of the airport and without which it would cease to exist; and sequence after sequence of fighters springing up in a tumult of noise that blasted aside the rain sounds and made conversation impossible for the moments of the jet takeoffs. Seeing, hearing, feeling this frenzy of activity, I felt no sense of intimacy toward Saigon. It seemed remote and tragic. And despite the miracle of American air power rushing at you from every direction, there was a menace in the atmosphere such as you find in an airport right after a plane has crashed and there is nothing more to do.

But there was warmth in the face of a friend who was waiting at the bottom of the steps. He was dressed informally, in short-sleeved shirt and slacks, and his thinning hair was wet from the rain. I was dressed formally because any journey is a reason to look as though you are going happily from one scene to the next — at least this is a rule I follow — and now in Saigon I had come to the end of one journey, and I was starting another, and there was no discomfort in the few wrinkles of a seersucker suit. But there was curiosity and wry amusement in the face of my friend. He made an amused reference to my formal dress. "You'll soon learn better," he said, as we went into the customs building.

I remembered the building from 1950 when I had first visited Saigon as a correspondent for *Time-Life*. Then, the French inspectors did not miss a thing as they went through your luggage, looking for weapons or documents and literature that would identify a correspondent as sympathetic to Ho Chi Minh. The French possessed customs. Their people, French from France, ruled the customs and the immigrations, and the only Vietnamese around then were a few flunkies who were no more than ornaments to the French rule that had as its supreme puppet the Emperor Bao Dai. Coming into Saigon in 1950 was simply coming into a part of France, not the France that inspires the heart and the intellect, but the France of discomfort, of a cruel quality that has no heart and that at any moment is transfigured by a mildewed attitude that assumes enemies are on all sides. For Vietnam in 1950 was an invention of this French sickness that refuses to accept what has happened — the Fall of France and the courage and the grace, intellectual and physical, of the Free French and the Maquis, and the voices of harmony that surrounded the resurrection of the French spirit in the days of the occupation. But none of this, none of the brilliance of a Malraux or a Sartre or a Camus pervaded the Vietnam of 1950. To the French it was still Indochina, and by their calculations, it would remain so. They had slipped in through either the collusions or the ignorance of the British, and they longed to wipe out the disasters of their World War II behavior with a storm of military victories against the insurrection; or rather, they were not willing to believe in the capacity of the Vietnamese people to erase France's image off the slate of Vietnam's current history. They scornfully called the Vietnamese *the yellows,* attributing to the people of Vietnam the inferiority of a lesser race. The French were the supreme and the consecrated; and everything about the superficial part of entering the airport in 1950 consisted of this attitude. The French inspected and stamped your passport. To get into the country then involved all kinds of security clearance before an American, especially a journalist, could get an entrance visa. But even though the French existed there on the surface, it was apparent that they had not recovered their former complete position of authority as rulers of Vietnam. And they would never recover it. For besides them, there was another power in the country, the Democratic Republic of Vietnam led by Ho Chi Minh, who was no longer talking and acting as a neutralist. He had by 1950, after five years of waiting for some sign that a neutralist line would pay off, definitely and openly announced himself a Communist. His government had been recognized by the Soviet Union, and the new power to the north, the Communist Chinese regime in Peking. The puppet emperor, Bao Dai, was remote from the people he supposedly led and loved; his life was framed within the confines of the mountain resort city of Dalat, the opium, the women, and the gay life the French led him to and beat upon him so that he was senseless to decide or see anything beyond which new diversion would break the daily boredom of belonging to the French. Ho Chi Minh had advised his people that discipline from the opiates of alcohol and opium supplied by the French were required to make a victory of the present.

The French were sheltering themselves behind the American need of France in NATO in western Europe. The result was that by the fall of 1950, Ho Chi Minh was attacking the Americans with the same vigor and venom he applied to the French. Ho had waited for some sign from the United States, but he had received none; nor had he had any significant encouragement from any western European nation. In fact, his greatest help immediately after World War II came from the government of Chiang Kai-shek, who had occupied the North after the Second World War, just as the British had the South. Occupying the North was something of a sop for Chiang Kai-shek, who like De Gaulle sat in on the councils of the Big Three as something of a poor country cousin who has to be recognized from time to time, whose presence is noted, and whose leave-taking is granted. But Chiang Kai-shek's army in North Vietnam had recognized the government of Ho Chi Minh, a government that had declared itself for all of Vietnam. The French reemergence in the South was precisely where the French preferred to start. Cochin China, the area of the South around and near Saigon, is the most valuable of all; 60 percent of French commercial interests made their profits in Cochin China. But though the South was an underground fief of the Ho Chi Minh forces, exacting taxes, spreading its message of revolution, the French did have some measure of control there. They were akin to an occupying force, fighting against an unseen army that was in their midst but could not be detected, because it wore no uniforms. It lived by Ho Chi Minh's adage that liberation of Vietnam would be achieved only through patience and bloodshed. And Ho Chi Minh had plenty of time. The French did not. For their participation in what the United States considered paramount, the North Atlantic Treaty Organization, France had in one way or another compromised American policy in Southeast Asia, notably in Vietnam. The United States remained silent when it could, offering fatuous platitudes that it wanted peace in Vietnam; but more often, as the late forties went by and 1950 began, the United States was forced into openly siding and identifying with and supporting the French colonial role in Vietnam. The United States tried to start its aid program through direct channels with the Vietnamese government of Emperor Bao Dai. But any accurate reporting from American diplomatic people in Vietnam told Washington that there was no government of Bao Dai that could efficiently and expeditiously funnel American aid into the hands of the Vietnamese people. It had to be done through the French. Then, when the United States found itself fighting the Chinese Communists in Korea, the American identification with the French role in Vietnam became a common crusade against Communism, in Korea and in Vietnam.

As for the physical presence of America in Vietnam in 1950, it was largely unseen. But you could taste it; there were American weapons on the French soldiers heading to the North, where the French were trying to pin down the army of Ho Chi Minh, which now had the sanctuary of the Chinese Communists at its back. You could also feel a question in the eyes of the French customs officials — were you an American who was ready to give the French everything, or were you one of the suspicious ones who wanted to talk to the Vietnamese? There were questions that were like an examination in political hygiene; offered casually even over an aperitif by the *suréte* police who questioned you before you were cleared to enter Saigon. What does Monsieur think of the Chinese Communists? Did Monsieur have any thoughts on that rascal Ho Chi Minh? Ah! Monsieur had written in his form that he intended to visit the North, and for what reason? It was polite, yet sickening because you knew that the war in Korea was something real that involved a clear principle, but that the war in Vietnam was not *our* war. But the French were drawing us into it with the same malevolent look one sees in the eyes of the man who comes up to you on the Rue de Rivoli offering filthy pictures and an exhibition.

✿

So it was then, but now the French had disappeared. There were Vietnamese officials behind the counters, and they spoke a shy English and an excellent French. They were harried, and the American passport was enough; no visa was immediately necessary, and the inspection of our luggage was cursory and polite. And everywhere there were Americans. They were in uniform and they looked bigger and healthier and younger and more innocent than the French of 1950 who were by and large a motley group, drawn from the colonial armies of Algeria and Senegal, and composed of many former German soldiers who took a tour in Vietnam rather than imprisonment or whatever other fate the French had in mind for them. They were a fiction of an army because they were living a fiction; they had been assembled to fight an enemy in Vietnam that had raised its revolutionary banner fighting one of the enemy, the Japanese member of the Axis. But the Americans were not a fiction. And what made it clear that moment was an American woman who had been on the plane from Bangkok, bringing with her a little boy of three. The father, who was an American Air Force officer, rushed to put his arms around the little boy, who was hiding behind his mother's skirts, tears and screams of terror coming from his lips because he didn't know the strange man in the uniform. And the woman looked at her husband — a wife who had violated orders to come and see her husband and return on the same plane to Bangkok an hour later. What I read in her face was that all three of them forcibly were part of something they had never asked for and never wanted. These were days they would rather not be living, and looking at them, I couldn't help thinking, the French *wanted* to be here, and they had lost.

Saigon had become a victim of changing times. That was the first impression I had as we drove from the airport into the city. Misfortune appeared everywhere, gutters filled with trash and garbage, and the slow painful course of the traffic, far more intense and noisy than I had expected. A generation earlier when the French had laid out the plan for the streets they had envisioned a small neat Paris. But it was now an effort to break through the mass of pedicabs and people that surged through the street in a perpetual and massive traffic jam. The vibrations of war echoed in the high-caged look in front of the restaurants and shops. There were people comfortably seated behind the heavy wire mesh, and it took only a few seconds to realize that the screen was there to protect them from hand grenades or bombs. Sometimes there were jeeploads of soldiers in steel helmets and holding rifles, and the closer we got into town, the more commonplace the sight of the Vietnamese soldiers. I wanted to know whether there had been any terror incidents in the last few days, and my friend, with a half-bitter laugh that I soon realized passed for bravado on the part of everyone who had been in Vietnam for a while, said, "Oh yes, there's been a killing or two. Nothing to worry about. Quite a sight, isn't it? All these guys on the cyclos. They wouldn't mind throwing a bomb or two at us, mow down a few more Americans to make us realize they're around." We sat back silent. The scents of Saigon were strong, smells of stagnant water, and then, less offensive, the strange sharp sweet-sour odors of the food. We could see people sitting beneath naked light bulbs, squatted down over a steaming pan of rice, their eyes on the cup they were holding in one hand, the other working the chopsticks. Each person seemed lost in the business of eating, oblivious to anything else but the food and whatever dream was in his mind. They covered the pavements, and somehow there was some kind of order there, but the traffic was a jostling channel of slow movement toward the heart of the city. On Cong Le the high trees arched overhead, and through the gap I could make out the cathedral and the flashing signs of numerous bars, at least twenty or thirty of them, tiny places that tried to make themselves alluring and wicked and potent with names like *Miami, Beatles, Suzanne.* Then suddenly the traffic opened up, and we were moving faster and the car brought us to the entrance of the Hotel Caravelle.

Across the street was the Hotel Continental, with its name large and black, and its look a memory of the French days, a surviving institution of French courtesies still remaining in Saigon. The Caravelle was modern. You enter up a short flight of stairs into a small foyer, and in the main floor lobby, which is attractive because it is light, everyone standing in front of the reception desk, or sitting in the chairs by the window crisscrossed with tapes for protection from flying glass should a bomb explode outside, suggests a secret. The people in the Caravelle, the guests, or the ones trying to get a room, are identified with importance. Every day they devote themselves to some aspect of the war; either they are correspondents, or military men, or visiting VIP's. There is none of the old-world charm of the Continental about the Caravelle. People come there begging for rooms every day, and the Vietnamese standing behind the front desk are in perpetual contest with the insoluble problem of having too many people and not enough rooms. I was lucky. I had a room.

❋

I met friends in the bar on the eighth floor — that famous bar that one had read so much about — where newsmen gathered, and reacted, and argued, and wrote their stories. Somehow the Caravelle bar was associated in my mind with one of the important facts of Saigon life. I remembered having read somewhere that when news of any importance broke in Saigon it was in the bar. Newsmen gathered like some secret clan in the bar before they raced off to write their stories. I expected to walk into it, and find myself in the midst of some honeycomb of activity and discussion. My disappointment was immense to walk in and find the room very small and darkly lit, with a tiny semi-circular bar where there was a short fat man saying something in a large voice.

He was certainly not making much of an impression on anyone except the one man sitting on the bar stool next to his. There was no mystery about the place. It was a refuge from tedium. It was what a bar should be — a place to have a drink. There was no hidden mystique to be discovered here, I was thinking to myself. Then someone said the fat man was Jimmy Breslin of the *Herald Tribune*, and again I felt disappointment. I had admired Jimmy's columns, but I had imagined him thin and nervous — and the man I now was introduced to was contrary to that image. He was fat, almost as if he were immobile, and couldn't move around very much, and certainly not fast. His eyes were what gave him away. They were dark and luminous and they contained the curiosity and the wisdom, the bitter intelligent wit that makes a Breslin column what it is. Then he began talking in a whirlpool of adjectives, speaking of Vietnam. This was the first glimpse that I had had from a member of the press corps as to what was happening in Vietnam; Jimmy in the darkness of the fabled Caravelle bar said it was awful, and he said it, moreover, as if he had a headache and a heartache. Then, silent, Jimmy drank his drink like a fugitive from a life he understood.

✻

That night at dinner in a Chinese restaurant in Cholon I was able to separate myself from the Saigon of my past. The reality of today's Saigon became visible in the glow of the flares over the city not far away, illuminating some lone sentry who needed the artificial light to make the night go faster. Of course, in that long ago of 1950, I had seen Saigon as a larger city. Now it had shrunk. The dominant mood of Saigon then was that the sun was shining again on France, and the importance of Vietnam was its economic value to Paris. In that distant France, Vietnam was a necessity for its moneys, for its land, for its prestige. Whatever might be the rights of the individual in Vietnam they were second to the rights of the Frenchman with an interest in increasing his fortune. There was something optimistic about the French in Vietnam in 1950. They were anxious to establish their rights, as they had been before the Second World War. If men like Ho Chi Minh got into the way of French aspirations for a postwar Vietnam, they were not understood, and they were to be pushed aside or destroyed. And the French went about Vietnam as professional soldiers out to war against anyone who stood in their way. They were not interested in injustice. They were absorbed in themselves.

We sat inside a comfortable restaurant with drinks that were excellent, and outside there was a sudden downpour of rain. The intense drumming sound and the large splashes sent the people scurrying back out of sight into places where they could keep dry. The empty street looked like something unknown. Saigon is people, and without them, it ceases to exist. We talked about this. By now a large number of friends were sitting at our table. They were all newsmen, and we knew each other from other countries and other stories; but those were forgotten now because once in Vietnam, there is nothing else to talk about. The country, the people, the war are all absorbing to a point that is almost excessive. Nothing else matters, and this tremendous involvement never ceases. There were candles on the table; the power had gone off as it does almost every day in Saigon. The food was delicious, Chinese, past criticism and worthy of the praise it received as we devoured it.

It was unusually peaceful and pleasant. But then I reminded myself that's how it had been before. The city was filled with the French Army, and there were many attractive French women. How different it was now. American women, except for those involved in the news business or employees of the embassy or the big construction companies like Morrison-Knudsen, could not come to Vietnam. In the French days, the French had kept their women in the country, no matter what the dangers. They half believed that it was going well for them, as even now we Americans were saying that with such a large buildup of troops in Vietnam, and with President Johnson so determined to see it through, there was no question that the war would get better. But it had gotten bad enough for us to send the American wives and children of the large embassy staff out of the country.

We talked of just where we stood. The Viet Cong were dominant throughout the countryside. Even the city of Saigon was under their influence. There were businesses in town that paid two taxes: one to the government of Premier Ky, and another to the Viet Cong who functioned in the city underground. And as we talked I tried to gather my thoughts back to what had finally sent the French out of Vietnam, and how we had gotten involved in Vietnam. In 1950, there had been considerable aid provided for the French Army, which we felt was supporting the southern axis of Asia, while we fought in Korea. Then the French defeat at Dien Bien Phu came into the conversation, and I remembered meeting the commander of the garrison, Colonel Christian de Castries. When I knew him he commanded a Moroccan battalion of infantry, and I had been on a number of sweep-and-clear operations with them in the North. The behavior of the French had fascinated me; they went out looking for the enemy, inviting him to attack, and they seldom made contact. You began to feel that there was no Viet Minh until one night they would attack and overrun one of the outposts the French maintained in outnumbered isolation in the middle of enemy-dominated terrain. The French had a suicidal outlook in one respect; they believed they were destined to die far away from home in Vietnam in order to answer those who had found their performance against Hitler's armies less than heroic. Colonel de Castries was a romantic. He was a proud cavalry officer, and he still talked of how a French cavalry officer won his spurs by going through a decathlon of a final examination in the field that tested his horsemanship, his swordsmanship. One of the more delightful aspects of the obstacle course was that he had to drink a magnum of champagne and service a well-experienced prostitute to her satisfaction, all in a half hour's time. Colonel de Castries was fond of his Moroccans; he permitted young Vietnamese boys to go with them, ostensibly as kitchen help, but at night they slept with the soldiers. Colonel de Castries reasoned they had to have something to keep up their spirits, just as he had a white horse trailing along the column to remind himself that he was still a cavalry man. And besides, the Colonel knew that the Viet Minh treated Moroccans badly. When they captured them, they were tortured cruelly because the Viet Minh had no pity for colonial peoples fighting them in their anti-colonial war. That war ended in Geneva four years later, in 1954, and I still remember seeing the Chinese Communists and the Viet Minh delegations arriving in their planes, and I remember the moment France's Foreign Minister Georges Bidault nearly broke down as he described the fall of Dien Bien Phu. The Geneva Conference also marked the end of France in Vietnam, and the real beginning of American participation. The United States was lined up supporting the government of Bao Dai, the dissolute emperor of a nonexistent nation. The actual Geneva Agreement was signed by Brigadier General Henri Delteil, of the French Army High Command, and Brigadier General Ta Quang Buu of the Viet Minh Army. When General Ta Quang Buu suggested a champagne toast to the French general, he was turned down. General Delteil said: "I am sure that you understand that this is not possible." The agreement was a military solution. It ended the fighting between the Army of France and the army of Ho Chi Minh. A gentlemen's agreement was made that elections would be held by 1956, but there was no document signed to that effect. It was a verbal promise. What Geneva did was to split the country at the seventeenth parallel. For all practical purposes, the South Vietnam we know today was born on July 21, 1954, when the French agreed to end the war. North Vietnam was for the first time recognized as an existing functioning nation by the French. Just as the United States does not officially admit to the existence of Chinese Communists, so the French for nine years had fought an army and a government that they had never considered legal. Yet when the time came for the French to get out of the war, they had to accept and recognize that the only party who could officially agree with them to end the hostilities was the same party who up until Geneva had not existed in the eyes of Paris. No wonder that the French had no time for champagne toasts at Geneva. They had lost a quarter of a million men in the war; the United States had spent one billion dollars supporting France in the war. The Vietnamese National Army, created throughout Vietnam, had 200,000 men. The French Army had been beaten by the Viet Minh, who had started fighting in 1945 with a small inferior arsenal; by the time of Geneva, the army of Ho Chi Minh was equipped with American weapons given to them by the Chinese Communists who had picked them up in the Korean War. The United States role at Geneva was largely that of listener-observer, though just before the conference was adjourned, the United States delegate, General Walter Bedell Smith, said that the United States would view any renewal of the aggression in Vietnam, in violation of the Geneva agreement, with grave concern. The words were important because the United States had already seriously considered direct intervention in the Vietnam war in support of the beleaguered French garrison at Dien Bien Phu. Secretary of State John Foster Dulles had told the French that we were ready to do so, and President Dwight D. Eisenhower had prepared the nation for American planes attacking the Viet Minh at Dien Bien Phu in a press conference on April 7, 1954, when he used the "domino theory" approach to justify American intervention. There was even serious thought of using atomic weapons. Vice-President Nixon had viewed the deteriorating situation at Dien Bien Phu as so serious that he had said the Eisenhower administration might have to send troops in order to save Vietnam from falling into Communist hands. Curiously enough, at that time Senator Lyndon Johnson, in a secret conference with John Foster Dulles, who was seeking support for American intervention, wanted to know who else besides the United States was willing to fight in Vietnam. Dulles said he had no other nation willing to go in with us. Today, as President, Lyndon Johnson does have token support for American participation — and American warplanes are daily hitting the airfield at Dien Bien Phu.

France physically left Vietnam three months before elections were to be scheduled. Hanoi wanted the French to stay because it was with France that Hanoi had signed the Geneva agreement. No one else present at Geneva was legally bound to see to it that the agreements made at Geneva would be fulfilled. Obviously to Hanoi, the crucial agreement was the elections. Anyone familiar with Vietnam then has sworn that in any such election Ho Chi Minh was certain to carry the entire country, thus reuniting the North and South under the banner of Communism. This was distinctly against the interests of the United States, who after Geneva, took over as the power behind the scenes in South Vietnam. The American choice was for Diem — and to every North Vietnamese proposal that some sort of normal communication between North and South be reestablished, such as roads, railways, and post offices, Diem turned a deaf ear. The seventeenth parallel became a wall between the North and South, and the higher it grew, the better the United States liked it. For immediately after Geneva, the United States policy, openly but more often covertly, was to do everything to strengthen the government of Diem. By now his contact with Emperor Bao Dai had been broken. He had completely assumed dictatorial powers. He had President Eisenhower's backing.

The White House had written Diem in October 1954, that the United States was ready to make an effective contribution in aid to the Diem government. He had gotten off to a good start — in the 300 days permitted by the Geneva agreement for free movement between North and South, 850,000 left the Communist North to come South — and a great many of them eventually found themselves in Saigon.

*

It is necessary to know Saigon if you are to know anything about South Vietnam. Each ripple on the surface of the city has meaning to every one of the sixteen million people who live in South Vietnam. The values that hold the nation together or tear it apart are characterized in the endless dimensions of Saigon today.

The towns and hamlets of Vietnam are its lifeblood, but Saigon is something different; for the Vietnamese, it is the town of dreams. Saigon was discovered by the Europeans. They made it, and no matter what happens in Vietnam, you can be certain that all roads finally lead to Saigon. When the French expeditionary force marched through its streets for the last time in 1954, they did it with tears in their eyes, singing a plaintive song that the love affair was over. Saigon is a love affair. Everyone wants a part of it. There is no single word that can describe her, for she is plain and bare and beautiful and ugly and cruel and dirty; people have died in her dehumanizing atmosphere; they have been drugged with the city and inspired in it, and yet that doesn't describe all of Saigon. The streets are passages of humanity, the windows of the houses are more often closed than open because it is hot most of the time and shade is necessary. The materials of war and of peace are to be found in the streets of Saigon: barbed wire and banks of flowers; rifles and the latest records of the Beatles and the Rolling Stones; grotesque carvings and delicate ancient coins a thousand years old; lovely girls with long dark hair, wearing the traditional white gown split at the waist and showing beneath the tight-fitting pantaloons that cling close to their bodies. The GI's call this the city of the VPL, the visible panty line. The girls, whether they are the good unapproachables or the ones found in the bars, resemble in delicacy and slenderness the tiny souvenir dolls sold at every street corner — the dolls that were rumored to be filled with an explosive charge put in them by the Viet Cong so that the souvenir would explode when it got back home to the living room, and kill mom, or sister, or sweetheart, twelve thousand miles away from Vietnam. The rumor, like the hundreds of rumors that beguile Saigon day in and day out, probably had an element of truth; but for the most part, the dolls are safe, though the people selling them have no beauty left in their faces. They sit in the winding noisy lanes, or on the wide and still more noisy boulevards, immobile, morose, waiting for a customer; and when they see him, they shout, "Number one, number one, doll." Every prospective customer, whether buying a package of black-market cigarettes, or a beer in a bar, hears the same old refrain of number one, and when a purchase is refused, a tip denied, the number one becomes number ten. Something like a curse falls upon the person who is a number ten. And there is an air of injury now in the voice that calls you a number ten; but injury is chronic in Saigon.

There is no distinctive building, no architecture that is intense and abundant, that takes you into its confidence and makes you open your eyes wider with the genius and eloquence of its stone and design. One building, a recent one, reveals much about Saigon's unpredictable, coup-prone governments. It stands in the center of town, encircled by a high iron fence. Above its facade and surrounding grounds is a spent air of gloom. It seems isolated and left over, like a pavillion at the World's Fair that Robert Moses can't get rid of for love or money. The building is in fact empty. It was erected for Premier Ngo Dinh Diem and, since his death, none of the succeeding premiers has wanted to live in it.

Survival is an instinct that is alive in everything in Saigon. Young boys of nine and ten work and hustle the streets, waiting for a sucker of a GI to come along, or a billfold to be picked (one tailor advertises pants with pockets that can't be picked). The same casual air is found in the teeming markets where one easily purchases American equipment and supplies that have been stolen that morning from the waterfront. And if they don't have your size in boots or a poncho, or whatever it is you want, they will get it — custom-made robbery. Everyone is helpful in Saigon, for a price. Anything can be organized. The essence of Saigon street society is a witches' Sabbath of convenience; no erotic desire is beyond finding. There are no pretenses. Life is feverish and monstrous; the misshapen bodies that cling to one are a part of the world of Saigon. The beaten survivors of the war, the disillusioned and homeless are everywhere with a frequency of numbers that reaches out at you, hotter than the air filled with all the noxious fumes of a traffic that creates a ground smog, more terrible than the stealing and cheating rampant everywhere. Saigon is a startling collection of the human and the inhuman. The city's population grows every day, a penniless influx that comprehends only one fact — that something good might happen in Saigon. They have run away from the war, from the villages and the land where they belong. Few of them possess anything when they come; and what they find is the life on the streets, where the guiding rule is if you don't take advantage of the first sucker, he will take advantage of you. Experience comes easy. The GI's come into Saigon, looking for escape and release from the war. They linger wherever there is an appreciative smile, and the younger the smiling face, the more the GI values the child, not knowing what lies behind the "Hello, Joe," the young fingers plucking at his sleeve, the chorus of "Number one, you number one." The American is not seen with awe, reverence, or even simple respect. He is someone better off. He can afford whatever it costs him to have a child's smile for a day, or a girl's body for a night. There is no sympathy. No bond. There is no contact, moral or spiritual or actual on any level, between the street society of Saigon and the men who come into the city to find quiet. For Saigon is frantic with struggle. Pity has escaped the soul of this city's people. You can buy pity from them; but they will never give it to you. And that is the unhappiness of Saigon. The city has a disturbing element, deceit has become part of the life of its people, and it becomes more pronounced as the war goes on and disillusion is based on every street corner.

2. PATROL

THE RAIN BEGAN TO FALL fifteen minutes before the platoon was to move out, and the lieutenant who was to be the leader winced as he felt the first drops fall on the map. He folded the map quickly and put it inside the waterproof case. A pained expression was in his eyes because of the injustice of the rain's coming now. He swore to himself. He was a young man of twenty-three from northern California who had been in the United States Marines for six months before coming to Vietnam. He had not shaved for three days and this gave his face a tougher harder look and his eyes a vigilant squint. The captain of his company slapped the lieutenant on the back. There was perhaps four or five years' difference in their ages, but the captain looked much older. We were sitting just outside a bunker that was dug deep underground and buttressed with sandbags. It looked like something out of the First World War. There had been rain for a number of days, and it had seeped down through the roof; the sandbags and the dirt floor were thoroughly damp, as if the bunker were a dungeon. I shook hands with the captain, and then I gave him my little package of identity cards, money, pictures, the few things that identified me with some other life somewhere else. They were all in a transparent waterproof tobacco pouch that was the best means I had found for carrying valuables in Vietnam. I gave them to him without any premonition that I would never see them again. It was the routine. You went out on a patrol into enemy territory and it was customary that you took with you only what was absolutely necessary.

The captain who took my wallet, and the sergeant who took the wallets from the men going out on the patrol didn't say anything about how long they would keep them, or what the disposition would be if the owners didn't show up to claim them. Nobody spoke about the future, of death or life. The patrol and whatever might happen to it had been discussed in detail. The Marines are thorough that way. They went out on patrols almost daily, and an NBC cameraman and I were going with them. Facts are the substance of any reporter; in our case, serving television news, facts had to be seen on film. There was no other way to get a story except to go where facts were made. A Marine patrol in the northernmost sector of South Vietnam was a legitimate fact of the war that had to be shown.

As we passed through the bivouac, on the way out of the safety of the perimeter with its fixed positions, its mortars, and its machine guns, and the sandbags and the men, an entire U.S. Marine company, I felt a sense of ritual. The Marines staying behind cast looks at us to see who was going. They displayed a professional appraisal of how men carried their weapons, and there was the same implacable air I have noticed at football games when the men on the bench watch the men on the field during a time-out. On the surface, there is an apparent lack of concern, but deep down, if you look closely into the eyes of the men watching, they are following every gesture very carefully, as if a part of themselves is also involved with the men going out on patrol. There is no pomp, no noise, but there was that day, for us, the rain. The first drops were cold, and there was a murmurous undercurrent as men reacted to the touch of the rain on their skins. No large sound. But you felt it more than you heard it; and then as the rain kept coming down, it was part of the patrol, and any objection your inner self felt to the wetness died down. The men's uniforms became darker. They wore no insignia. The packs were light, and around them were black stockings filled with C-rations which were pressed closely together making the stockings look like enormous sausages. The weight was the ammunition. Two hundred rounds per rifleman; two to four grenades per man. The machine-gun teams carried the bandoliers of the thirty-caliber ammunition strung across their chests like bandits of a Pancho Villa gang. Incongruously, as we moved out, we did not go across a field; we headed down a highway. A two-lane asphalt road that had a surprising amount of civilian traffic, small busses overloaded with people looking at us as we marched by on foot. A long way off, diagonally distant from the road was the jungle, the shelter of the enemy. Experience had taught the Marines not to head directly into it, but choose their point of entry from an angle that is unexpected and where they will least be observed. You cannot conceal much in Vietnam; but there are ways of safeguarding lives, and ways of endangering them. We were hedging toward the jungle, a safer course than moving directly to it. The lives of the civilian population in the fields seemed to bear no relationship to us except that they saw their duty as work in the fields; ours to find the enemy. The Marines towered over the people who sometimes stood at the side of the road. They did not come near us; and between the Marines, talking began.

"You think these goddamned people just happen to be here, do ya?"

"Yeah, they countin' us. You wait, we'll hear them drums soonuff."

"Shut it up," snarled a sergeant.

"Ain't it the truth though, sarge. Ain't it?"

The sergeant said, "Sure it is. But keep your fuckin' mouth shut."

So there was silence again, and the wet Marine faces kept looking around, eyes fixed on nothing special, taking in everything, getting the sense of the land; but annoyance remained in their look. They didn't trust the people. There's something wrong-feeling about going out on a patrol with civilians looking at you, knowing that you are out, feigning that they are not interested, but you know that they are. "Hell, what kind of a fuckin' war is this?" mutters a Negro sergeant to himself. I was walking ahead of him, and I looked back over my shoulder to see him. His eyes met mine, he smiled, and whispered, "Why don't you carry a weapon?" I told him that it's just another piece of equipment. Taking movie cameras and sound equipment into the field is load enough. We carry our own rations, and extra film, and I'm lazy. The less I carry the better I like it.

He said, "If I were a civilian and I didn't have to be here, no amount of money would ever get me out here." Then he wanted to know if I carried a lot of insurance, and I said not enough for what I think I'm worth, and he laughed and said, "Ain't that the truth."

Then we broke off from the road, and we traveled across a rice field, and the rain was lighter. We move faster now, and almost naturally we take advantage of the cover and keep the distance between us wide, because the more far apart we are from one another the less tempting a target we make. We know where the man in front of us and the man behind us are, but the rest of the platoon is out of sight. The radioman was ahead of me, and he put down his aerial so it wouldn't stick up and point him out. He turned his head and he beckoned me closer and he said, "You oughtn't to be with me. They always go for the radioman." And I asked him why and he looked at me as if I had said something wrong or stupid, but I wanted to hear his answer.

He said patiently, "They get the radio and we can't call in the planes to hit them. Unnerstan?" And I said to him that I'd like to stick with him because his will be the only sound on the patrol, unless we get into a fight. Sound is one of the facts it's my job to record. "Okay, buddy," he says, "but you look careful, won't you?"

Once you're with soldiers like this, you don't have to worry about their posing or faking for pictures. They don't look at you, they don't think about you as being a correspondent. You are with them on the patrol, and that's the only job they're concerned about — the patrol. You've been included in. They don't even remember your name. But for however long the patrol lasts, you are one of them.

This was my first time with the Marines, and the aspect that interested me most was their conduct on these patrols. I had just arrived in Vietnam, and there had been considerable comment and furor over a television report by Moreley Safer of CBS News that the Marines were going about the countryside burning villages and leaving people homeless, that their first thought was to destroy whatever crossed their path without discrimination. It wasn't part of my job to answer the CBS report. In the highly competitive and often savage duels between the networks, one didn't dignify the other by doing a follow-up on their story. From the NBC point of view, I was on the patrol to report what happened. But as a reporter and as an American, I was interested in how the Marines did handle themselves. The Safer account had been something of a disaster for the Marines' public image, and their attitude toward newsmen, immediately after the Safer episode, was one of caution. This did not mean that the Marines had tried to prevent me or anyone accredited to the Military Assistance Command in Viet Nam from covering their activities; far from it, as far as the Marine Corps was concerned, a reporter could go anywhere, no matter how dangerous. If you wanted to be in the point of a patrol, you would be placed there. (I hadn't asked for it, and I never would.) I had seen plenty of action as a soldier and as a reporter. I had nothing to prove to myself or anyone else about myself and war. And I knew better than to go into a point with the Marines, or anyone else in Vietnam.

Men get killed at the point surer and faster than anyone else; and yet men volunteer to lead the platoon, to be the first men out front, the scouts, the bait, the men the enemy sees first. They do it because there is a legend that it's safer at the point, on the theory that the enemy won't shoot at the point first, but will let it go by to get the main body. They also volunteer to be the point because they want to prove something about their courage. It's not surprising to find the meekest-looking men at the point. As it happened on this Marine patrol, at the point were young men in their teens. Despite their youth, they were sure of themselves. This was not their first patrol; they had survived others. On our first break, just prior to entering the jungle, I went up forward to see them. Their rifles were in their laps, each man had one hand on his gun, and in his free hand, a cigarette. They were staring out at the jungle, just ahead. The sight of the jungle is never comforting. It's a deep, dark, green retreat, shrouded in silence, adding to the sense that it is a haven for someone else, namely the enemy, but not you.

"It looks like a fuckin' wall," said one of the Marine scouts. He had rubbed mud on his face to hide the pinkness of his skin. I wondered whether he shaved.

The men of the point were sitting close together like conspirators, and as I came closer to them they made room for me. No introductions were necessary. They knew reporters were on the patrol, and they had no occasion to ask me more. Their greeting was to make room for me among them, and to silently offer a cigarette.

I took a light from one of their cigarettes. You don't use matches unless you have to, and as long as someone has a cigarette going, you share that light. That's part of a patrol's life, too — the way men want to light cigarettes from one another. It's a kind of embrace, embodying in the action a familiarity, a friendship.

"Shit," said another Marine.

"Shit what?" said his buddy.

"I gotta get me some kindofa souvenir."

"Yeah?"

"What kind of motherfuckin' souvenir you talkin' about?"

"I mean a million-dollar wound."

"Yah, like right up your asshole."

"Naw. You know what I mean. Nothin' that hurts much. Nothin' that screws you up from makin' it with a broad."

"Yeah. Like right between your motherfuckin' eyes."

"I dunno. I heard about that Marine that got it in the leg, and they didn' haveta operate or anything but it got complication an' they hadta send him back to the States and he's gonna getta leave and then he's gonna make corporal and shit, the guy gotta million-dollar wound. That's what I want."

"You keep wishin' boy and you'll get a fuckin' million-dollar zap up the asshole . . ."

They didn't laugh. They were content to talk about it the way college freshmen sit around a bull session, captives of their own language, occupied in expressing themselves without any possibility of censorship. The men of the point were natural. I had wanted to ask them how they felt, yet that would have been unnatural. I was glad to have heard what I did. I left them to go farther back, knowing that they were going into the jungle first.

✤

In Vietnam, as soon as you step into the jungle, everything is magnified. Nothing is eliminated. And you are alone. There is no talk. The shadows loom larger, and the light, if it can be called that, is a blemish that hides any movement around you. The imagination can fancy anything in the jungle. One leaf, rustling ever so slightly, can set every nerve in your body into shutting and opening with a movement so loud that you think everyone can hear and see your fear. The trees look taller and thicker and higher than any trees you've seen before. The tradition of the Viet Cong is to post a sniper in the trees, far enough away so that you can't see him, near enough so that he can send bullets down among you.

The jungle and its life is the presence; the men within the jungle, dwarfed by it, are the intruders. An infinity of growth, creepers, vines, bushes, trees, growing at all lengths, have no continuity, no form, because the jungle is living disorder. It gathers around you, in your nostrils, your brain, dulling you into a state of anguish. You cannot hurry through it because each aching step is an engagement where man is inferior to the growth. Each vine is a defending force that has to be cut bit by bit, through thorn and thickness that takes every opportunity to slow the men down. The jungle is something on a big scale, like some monster looking down through its magnifying glass at the men below, infinitesimal, trying to get through. And yet wherever men fight in Vietnam, the jungle is part of the battle; once in the jungle, one feels it perpetually as if it were the oppressor, an eternity whose tremendous power is against you. The jungle drives men mad because each step through it is a decision made in pain and sweat. And silence. A man cannot swear aloud. He cannot express his indignation in any way except as he swings his machete above his head, down onto a vine, cutting as through the arteries of something that will scream for mercy. Every man in Vietnam who has fought the jungle has, at one time or another, prayed for the enemy to appear. His despair with the jungle has been so great that he prefers someone human to fight. Men loathe the jungle. It kills courage. It brings out fear in every man.

I could not remember very much of how we got through, but late in the afternoon a sound came through the jungle that did not belong there. At first, I thought it was some monstrous bird beating its wings, and then as I tried to realize that it was a drumming sound, the Negro sergeant gave me the answer.

"Charlie and his fuckin' drums."

"Drums?" I said.

"Yeah. He knows we're comin'. His people back there on the road tole him and now he's passin' the word. They use the drums . . . talkin' drums like in Africa."

Now I could hear it as a drum.

"They going to attack?" I asked the sergeant.

"Sooner or later," he said. "But not right now. Charlie, he wants to make us sweat. He's a sly one."

The drums continued beating, sometimes sounding far away, then nearer. They stopped, and the silence of the jungle was a bombardment.

It didn't last long. The sniper fire began with only three shots, fired somewhere behind where I was standing. The radioman fell to the ground faster than I did. I looked around at the Negro sergeant. His gun was aimed up at the trees. Three more sounds of the Viet Cong rifle, and I listened to it, hearing it for the first time. It sounded slight, weak, as if it were not really fired from a rifle but made by hitting a couple of sticks together to make a clicking sound.

At this point, the radioman was talking into his handset, using the code language. The young lieutenant had joined him. There was the sound of one of our light machine guns firing.

"Goddamnit," said the lieutenant, "find out what the hell they're firing at."

The radioman talked his unintelligible language, and then he said to the lieutenant: "The point reports it's got one VCC KIA."

"Our guys okay?"

The radioman turned to the lieutenant: "They got the kid from Minneapolis."

The lieutenant showed no change of expression. He told me he was going forward and asked if I wanted to come along. I said I did. I hoped my cameraman would be there. We had gotten separated when the firing began. I also hoped that the kid from Minneapolis wasn't the one who wanted a million-dollar wound.

As we made our way up to the point, we moved in a crouched position, taking a few steps, stopping to listen, frozen, then running. The Marines sprawled out on the ground were positioned out, facing all directions. The sniper fire had stopped, but they were no less alert. Besides myself and the lieutenant, there was a third Marine, who kept close to us. He carried an M–14 rifle, and he was the lieutenant's bodyguard. The young officer had only a pistol at his waist, and it was still holstered. It took only a few minutes, five or six, to reach the point where a knot of men were clustered around two bodies spread-eagled on the ground. The lieutenant was furious.

He began spitting epithets; "Goddamnit," he said, "this is no fuckin' picnic. Spread out."

The Marines did so, but rather reluctantly. Death has a way of drawing men together. They were curious about the Viet Cong. And they wanted to look at the Marine, too. They were aware that the dead man on the ground might have been any other one of them, and they pondered the uncertainty and the bad luck that had made it this Marine's day to die. I stared down at his young face. The Navy corpsman had taken off his helmet, and his hair was brown. At first I wouldn't have recognized him as the kid who had wished for a million-dollar wound. Death had transformed his face so that it had no expression, though his twisted body, with one leg bent awkwardly under the other, still suggested the youthfulness and cocky assurance he had shown only an hour before. It was definitely the kid from Minneapolis. The helmet, lying nearby, had his name and that of his girlfriend written on the side. He had enclosed the two inside a heart.

The radioman had joined us, and the lieutenant told him to call in the company so that a chopper could come in and take out the dead Marine. I looked down at the Viet Cong. He was the first one I had ever seen. He wore a pair of black pajama bottoms, but his chest was bare. His hair was very long and dark, and his eyes were still open, with a look of transfixed outrage. His weapon had been taken from him. There was nothing to identify him as a soldier. His sandals were old and used, and there was little difference between him and thousands of peasants. The Marines had not been merciful. There were bullet holes all over his body, and the force of them had knocked him out of a tree.

They had found a VC flag on him. It was a yellow star on a red and blue field, and the Marines who had taken up positions on the ground not far away from us were arguing about who should get the flag. The lieutenant picked it up from the little pile of papers, wallet, and rifle with a bandolier of ammunition they had found on the enemy sniper. Behind him, one of the Marines called out: "Lieutenant, I should get to keep it. I hit him first."

"My ass you did," argued another Marine. "I started firing the same time you did, and I had him in my sights."

"I got him first."

"Knock it off," said the lieutenant. "No one's getting the flag. It goes back with me and I'm giving it to the Marine lieutenant who got wounded yesterday. I promised him he could have one if we found one."

"Aw, Christ, Lieutenant. You know the rules. If a guy wants a flag he has to come out here and get it himself."

"This is different," said the lieutenant. He named the Marine officer and he said that he had been wounded saving two of his men who had been pinned down. Anyway, he was the officer and he had his hands on the flag and that settled it. I looked at the

Marines to see if they looked rebellious, but they didn't. Later I heard from them that the Marine officer who had gotten wounded was a good guy and they didn't mind his owning the flag. The fact that he had saved two of his men was something they respected. They also admitted that they weren't sure who had killed the sniper first and there would have been hard feelings in the patrol against whoever wound up with the flag. This way it made them feel generous and big to make the flag a present to someone who deserved it, even though he wasn't with them. But he was a Marine, and Marines stick together. Besides, the officer was going back to the States with half his face shot off. Swearing secrecy, they admitted to me that when they dragged the dead VC over from the tree he had been shot out of, they had taken a small knife from his belt and not turned it in with the rest of the stuff. The knife would only be pocketed by some intelligence fat-cat back at Da Nang, and later they were going to settle who should keep it by throwing dice.

✻

We buried the dead VC where he had fallen, but we carried the body of the Marine for a half mile to a paddy field where the chopper was going to land. It was a wide field and there was jungle on all sides, but for anyone to get in to where we were, would have meant their being spotted long before they could reach us. The lieutenant felt it was a good place to bivouac for the night. It was drawing close to five o'clock in the afternoon, and the dark would fall in an hour.

The patrol knew that back at Da Nang, there were plenty of reenforcements, standing by to come in by chopper if we were hit. They had hoped to ambush the enemy in this area, but now we seriously doubted that such could be accomplished. It would be a mistake to suppose the VC did not know we were here. Tomorrow it would be a day's march back to the company bivouac. The only serious risk we ran was that the enemy might attack us at night. We had no intelligence that they were in this area in a large force, so if they did come, we would learn something. The lieutenant gave his orders as if he knew that we would indeed be attacked. He saw to it that the position was well protected with outposts on our flanks and the mortars and machine guns set up for the widest range over the approaches across the paddy field. The jungle was at a distance of a mile from the center of our perimeter. He called on base to order flare planes to fly over all night long so that if the enemy were to try and reach us, we had more than an even chance of seeing him. They were inviting the enemy to attack us. I was impressed with the Marines' willingness to take a calculated risk. None of the Marines failed to understand what was happening. They did not linger as they started digging in, knowing that the first sign of any significant attack would be mortars coming into our position. They dug deep holes. There was no confusion. Every man knew his job. When we had finally dug in, they lighted fires. There was nothing to hide. If the enemy didn't see our fires, he almost certainly would hear the chopper when it came in to get the dead Marine and bring us food supplies and water.

The helicopter put down quickly. On either side of it, still in the air, were the gunships, helicopters flying over the tops of the jungle forest, very low and very deadly. If there were enemy movement in there, they would unleash rockets and machine guns. They were the armor of the helicopter that unloaded the C-rations and the jerry-cans of water. The food was taken off and the dead man put on in a matter of minutes. The helicopter's rotor never stopped turning; the air around it was impatient. The pilots didn't want to waste time on the ground, and as soon as the body in its rubber sack was on the chopper, it was off and lost in the approaching gloom of night.

Now, the bivouac was suddenly quiet, Marines retiring into their holes to eat their supper of C-rations. There was little sound. This was the beginning of the long wait through the night. To a degree, we were exposed and lonely, and as night came on fast now, the air turned damp and unfriendly. The jungle seemed less distant. We were alone, fifty men clearly visible in a paddy field, encouraging the enemy to come at us.

All I had was a lightweight poncho and because my hole was damper than the ground above it, I spread the poncho out and lay on it. I had joined up with my cameraman, a Vietnamese named Nghia, and we had our holes near one of the machine guns. The lieutenant was going to make a round of the perimeter. It was too dark to film, but I went along with him. I could carry my tape recorder and take some of the conversation he had with his men on tape. But there was nothing to record. We went from hole to hole and nothing was said. He simply came up to the men, looked them over, and gave them a chance to see him, and then he went on. I got the impression that he wanted them to know he was there, and that he also was making mental notes of where each position was, and who was in it. Though there was silence throughout the whole inspection, there was a clear sense of communication between the lieutenant and his men. All the fires had been put out now and it was pitch dark. But the men smoked cigarettes. They hid the glow of the tips, not with any deliberate concern, but as a simple natural gesture.

Halfway around the perimeter, the first flare plane came over — it was a C-123, and you can always tell it because it makes such a buzzsaw of a sound. It dropped the first flare, and the area to our front was illuminated by an orange light, not quite the same as daylight, but bright enough so that if there were any perceptible movement on any scale it could have been seen. The C-123's appeared every three minutes — you could hear them coming and going — and they dropped the flares in perfect precision. Our position was not illuminated, but the area all around was.

I wondered as I returned to my hole whether I would be able to sleep. The drone of the planes and the subsequent almost continuous light was unfamiliar. Nghia was already sound asleep. I wondered whether we would get hit that night and if Nghia could film the shooting in the dark. Could I describe the fight on a tape recorder, at least my own impressions? I had to take a piss, but I was afraid to get up and go toward the outer perimeter because a Marine might shoot me. I didn't want to piss right near my own hole or the others around me. I decided to wait, and then I fell asleep, and much later I was awakened by the sound of machine-gun fire. Nghia was up, and I could hear the planes still overhead, and the flares still dropping . . .

"Goddamn it," said one of the Marines, shouting above the racket of the machine-gun fire. "It's just a kid."

"You're full of shit. All those VC are small. He's running around out there."

Then another burst of machine-gun fire.

"I got him that time. I got him," shouted the Marine.

I jumped into the hole with them.

"How many?" I said.

"Just one," said a Marine.

The Marine behind the machine gun looked up, bewildered.

"Out there," he pointed. "The son of a bitch is still out there. It can't be the same one."

"Your fuckin' A, it's the same fuckin' kid," said the other Marine.

I looked and it was a bizarre sight — a small silhouette of a boy, running around the paddy field, chasing after the sound of the C-123 above him, running as if he were flying a kite because his arms were raised and he seemed to be having fun. And then the tracers from the machine gun reached out for him like a distorted broken finger, and the kid danced away and fell to the ground. The drone of the plane continued and the new flare came down, and the little boy appeared again like a jumping jack, and he was chasing after the new sound of the plane as if he were caught up in an insane game of trying to leap up into the air after it. And this time the tracers of the machine gun reached him, and the boy fell, not as if he had chosen to fall in his wild hide-and-seek out there in the paddy field. The machine-gun bullets had killed him. I knew it. The machine gunner knew it, and the two Marines knew it. We looked out at the field, and the continuing illumination and we felt somehow as though we had witnessed something we didn't want to believe.

"I know it was a kid," said the same Marine.

The gunner looked at him, "Shut your fuckin' mouth. They've got decoys and they're small and the orders are clear. We kill anything that's moving out there."

The morning came and there was no mortar fire, no other shot fired through that night. We went out to where the body was and it was a little boy; he looked like eight, but he was probably twelve. The diet is poor in Vietnam and the bodies are smaller. He was lying face down in the wet paddy field, and the machine-gun bullets had practically chopped him in half. In his hand were the parachutes from the flares he had been collecting. We buried him and the epitaph was muttered by the Marine who had killed him. "This is a fuckin', lousy, shitty, dirty war."

*

The description was an accurate characterization of the war in Vietnam. It shocked the Americans who had to fight and die in it; and it shocked me. What was most disturbing about risking your life in Vietnam was that you were never certain why you were doing it. Men talked about fighting Communism when they were safely enough away from the front lines. Nobody talked about Communism where there was shooting and killing. It wasn't clear where the danger was or what we were trying to save — except our own lives. The GI's went forward to express their belief in their unit, in themselves. They recognized the Viet Cong as an opponent. They hated him for being out there ready to kill them if they made a mistake. The Americans who did the fighting knew they could count on the men who were part of their unit, the fire team, their platoon, their company. They didn't think about winning the war as much as they thought about doing the job they had to do and surviving for twelve months, when they would automatically go back home. At first, the GI's tried to make friends with the civilian populace. They wanted the people to love them for being there. They thought the people were against what they were against — the Viet Cong.

But as time went on, they found out that the people didn't care why the Americans were there. The Americans were as much an enemy as anything else. And this hurt the GI's. They were dismayed when the people attacked them, when they threw stones at a convoy going past, or planted a mine knowing for sure that it would blow up a truckload of GI's. They said, in their words, the people want to screw us any way they can.

Misfortune was commonest in the area where the First Corps of the U.S. Marines were based. It had been touched by war's misfortune for as long as people could remember. The policy of the individual Marine was a policy of getting the people to trust the Marines. There began a dual policy that would reveal the Marines not only as fighters, but as lovers of peace. The one policy was combat; the second involved a program that concerned itself with the welfare of the people. For the Marines realized early in the game, that at the root of all the trouble in Vietnam was a deep vein of dissatisfaction with the way things were.

*

Protection is akin to love; it is received only by those who want it. The U.S. Marines could not give away protection. The threat of betrayal by the local population constantly hangs over the Marines. They are in a tempest of discontent. They cannot storm ashore as they did in World War II's island-hopping campaign and win their objective. The problem in Vietnam is that objectives are obscure. There is a constant pessimism.

People believe that life revolves around war. Children have grown up in it. Rewards and punishments are concerned with battlefields. Injustice is established; justice is unknown. The truth is that people have lost understanding of any order, any life that is devoid of war. Betrayal is a legitimate road to victory.

The little boy who was killed by the Marines lived in a world of war. He had gone out in the paddy field at night, knowing that the flares were dropped by parachute. The parachute cloth represented life; the danger of venturing out where he would be killed was also a normal part of life. He was therefore not taking any undue chances when he set off to recover as much of the cloth as he could before daybreak. Had he gotten away safely, he would have been that much richer. Actually, he was being realistic by being there. His life ever since he had been born was fraught with different degrees of danger. There are tens of thousands of children who are orphaned from the moment they are conceived. There are more children unwanted in Vietnam than anywhere else in the world. India with all its widespread poverty and its Pandora's box of troubles has one blessing: the children never cry. The Indians would sooner die than see a child shed tears. Sociologists and psychologists who have ventured into India have been amazed by one compelling factor: that in all the immensity of India's poverty, there is no sign that the children suffer. The adults protect and nourish the child's innocence. Suffering is central to the adult world of India, but in Vietnam, suffering is the lot of the young. They inherit from the moment of birth all the immense loads of a country where forces of destruction prevail. A child born in Vietnam today inherits a land where there is no innocence.

❄

The patrol started back to the base bivouac without any appreciable change of mood. There was no further talk about the dead boy. Even if you started to think about him, you forced yourself to hide *that*. There was no obvious guilt. There is no room for any of that when you might be blown up by setting your foot in the wrong place. The truth of being in Vietnam is being in a war where spiritual heights are not apparent.

I had been told enough about the way the Viet Cong mined the trails, so I was walking to the side of the trail. Behind me, the same Negro sergeant, "You'd better mind where you're stepping. You keep on the trail." There was sympathy in his voice.

I looked back and saw he was walking dead smack up the trail, not much wider than a foot, and not clearly distinguished, but still a path over which many others had passed before us. I followed his example, and I kept up an over-the-shoulder conversation with him.

"But," I said, "I thought the trail was the most dangerous place."

"You kiddin'?" he said.

"No. I thought they put the booby traps in the trail."

"Shit, no. They gotta use the trail, and that's where they walk. So they like to put the booby traps along the side where they figure we might be walkin'."

I saw the logic in what he said. I told him that I would have my cameraman come up and film him as a kind of thanks for his keeping me alive.

"None of that television stuff for me," he said.

"Why not?" I said. "Your wife will see you on TV."

"Christ, no," he said. "I don't want her seeing me where I am now."

"How come?" I said.

" 'Cause I told her I got me a nice soft job. She don't know that I'm out here on patrols."

We reached the outskirts of a village, and the first thing we saw were the trenches. They were deep, fantastically well made, situated on the tree line, and they were extensive enough to have accommodated scores of troops — perhaps as many as two hundred men. Crossing over them was like penetrating a boundary line that the Viet Cong had set up against us. We were sure that the enemy wouldn't be in the village. They had run off, not wanting to fight on this day. I wondered what kind of a fight it would have been had they chosen to stay. They certainly would have killed some of us, because in their trenches they would have had the initial advantage until we had our planes coming in. I wondered what kind of men the Viet Cong were, and I had to admit to myself that it took courage to stay in those trenches waiting for the Americans, knowing that once the Viet Cong had committed themselves to a fight, they would be confronted with the awesome air power the Americans had at their beck and call. Sometimes it took only ten minutes from the time a call went out for the airplanes to arrive over the enemy and start pounding him. And the Viet Cong had no airplanes of their own. They were fighting with a number of disadvantages. But they felt they were winning and would win, no matter how many Americans, no matter how long it would take.

Marching into the village was ghostly. There was no activity of any kind. All the men had disappeared. There were only women and children huddled inside the drab huts with thatched roofs. The women kept their faces hidden behind their children's heads, and the children stared out at the Marines without so much as a murmur. The Marines went about their business of checking the village without paying any attention to the villagers, as if the village had been abandoned and there were no people in it. There were fires going on hearths in the huts, and the flame looked warm, but none of the Marines bothered the people or their fires. After they had checked out the village to see whether there was anyone hiding in the trench system under the houses, the Marines sat around outdoors to eat their C-rations. They ate them cold, and they kidded a little about how much time they had left in Vietnam, and whether their girls would be still waiting for them back home. They had in no way intimidated the villagers; on the contrary, it seemed to me that they had been very considerate of the people's privacy within their homes, going inside for a look, but not turning over things and creating havoc. They did not smile at the children, or even pay any of the usual attentions that so frequently characterize the GI attitude toward children.

I asked them what they felt about the people, and they said that if the people didn't harm them, they were not about to bother the people.

"Sure as hell," said one corporal, "they'll tell Victor Charlie all about us when he comes back. But what the hell, wouldn't you do the same if you were them?"

I looked at the other Marines, and saw no disagreement in their expressions. They were young, all in their late teens and not what could be called the professional Marine. This was their first experience with war. What interested me most was how calm they were about it all, accepting their role in Vietnam as something that had to happen. Now, resting in a small village where the enemy had slept the night before, they could understand the loyalties of the village women for their men. They were neither impressed nor depressed by this fact. They began talking about the Negro riots in the Watts section of Los Angeles. The Negro sergeant was there, listening.

"I wonder what it was turned them on," said one Marine.

"Whatever it was, they tore into everything. Shit, there's more war going on in L.A. than there is here in Vietnam."

"Sergeant?" I said to him. "What do you think about it all?"

He looked at me thoughtfully, and then he licked his lips, and he said, "They're no account. There's a right way and a wrong way. They took the wrong way. I think the Negro has his rights and he has to get them, but there wasn't any reason they had to cut up like crazy."

There was another young Negro private listening. In the Marines, a Negro is a Marine first. He is looked at and judged as a Marine. There was no sense of color among us as we sat there talking, but still the Negro private had something on his mind, and he was keeping it to himself.

Afterwards, when he had a chance to talk to me alone, he came up to me and said, "Listen, what the sergeant said that was okay, but I think you ought to know that I don't agree with him. I think the Negro has the right to protest any way he can — and if he has to start a riot like he did in L.A., then that's part of it, too, and you can't fault him for it. Understand, I think the sergeant was taking too easy a line, and I repeat, the Negro has a right to protest any way he wants to, if he's getting the dirty end of things. Hell, what am I here for if I didn't believe that?"

The more I saw of the Marines the more I became impressed with the success of their integration. The same was true of every military unit in Vietnam, but that was to come later. My first impression was that no one wanted or believed in segregation. There was something deeply human in the way men responded to each other, and trusted one another, without any reference to color. When it's not wanted, segregation disappears. The war in Vietnam had done at least one thing that we could be proud of — it had destroyed segregation.

Toward dusk, we reached the company bivouac. We came into the perimeter, as if we had been out on something routine. When the wallets were handed back to the men, they put them in their pockets without a word. There was hot food waiting, and they ate in silence. There was a report to be made to the captain by the lieutenant, and he gave it straightforwardly, without any drama or embellishments. The trenches of the village were marked out on a map so that the next patrol would know their whereabouts and not be caught off guard.

Then the lieutenant opened a can of beer, and sat down to write a letter to the parents of the dead boy from Minneapolis. It was the first one he had ever written, and his only problem was how to end it. He didn't want to say that he was sorry. He hated the word "condolences." He finally wrote, "I was proud to have him in my platoon. He never complained and he made a fine Marine." Then he signed his name, sealed the envelope, and went off to have his hot meal.

3. THE OTHER WAR

SIXTY MILES SOUTH of the great Marine base at Da Nang is a wide sandy stretch of area known as Chu Lai. Until the Marines got there, it was a barren place where an occasional fisherman might put in to avoid a storm. Hardly anybody cared about it except the Viet Cong who used it for training their people. I reached Chu Lai from Da Nang by C–130.

The first thing that struck me was the sand and the feverish activity everywhere. I was quite unprepared for so much work. The scene was reminiscent of something left over from World War II, with great earth-moving machinery grunting and roaring, and flying right above, screaming Marine Phantoms, disappearing into the sky carrying bomb loads. There was no way to get to Chu Lai except by air. The land between Chu Lai and Da Nang was controlled by the Viet Cong. Every hill, every piece of high ground was dominated by the Viet Cong, but here by the water, the Marines were building bases and airfields.

✳

My idea in coming to Chu Lai with cameraman Larry Travis was to see what the Marines were doing about the civilians caught in the war. How many it is impossible to estimate. But it is certainly tens and tens of thousands of people, possibly a million. It is also estimated that for every soldier who is killed in action, six civilians die. Could the Marines, who are trained for combat, attack a problem that involved non-combatants? The Marines' area of responsibility is densely populated, and almost every action involves civilians. Where there was combat there would be civilians. The Viet Cong knew this, and they spread the word that a Marine qualified for the Corps by killing his mother and raping little girls.

✳

Behind the vast military machine the United States had committed to Vietnam was something more important — proving that Americans were not about to destroy personal liberties. In fact, the people had to be taught that American presence enhanced the opportunities for liberty, and that the Viet Cong endangered them.

I spent a few days with the Second Battalion of the 7th Marines. They had covered themselves with glory in the first big operation of the American war in Vietnam, called Operation Starlight — where they had surrounded and destroyed a VC regiment — and now they were back in their base bivouac at Chu Lai. The Viet Cong were near, in the hills above, and every night they fired mortar shells into the camp.

Then the mortar attack would pass, and the rain-swept night remained. There were only the lights of our cigarettes as we sat in silhouette, talking. And the question I asked was, was this war like other wars, and the answer came from the battalion commander, Bull Fisher, who had been listening. He got up from his cot and he joined us, and this is what he said.

"We sent a patrol out today into an area that we have been patrolling for fifteen straight days. Today, we finally caught Charlie . . . we killed five of them. Make you no mistake about it, this war is different. This type of war takes time. I was on Iwo, we took that in twenty-six days. Tarawa in seventy-one hours. This is a different war. We have a defensive role. And we move out to assault and sweep and sweep and sweep. There is no such thing as a secure area. There is no such thing as a main line of resistance. Here it's a matter of enclaves and sweeps and pacification. The enemy will only fight when *he* wants to fight . . ."

I asked him what he thought was the basic factor in winning the war and he said, "In Vietnam, there are four main ingredients: the rifle, the machine gun, the mortar, and the man who uses them. All have changed since the Second World War except the mortar. The sixty-millimeter mortar is back in fashion. The rifleman is concerned with what is going on in his squad, his platoon; anything else is remote. The rifleman gets the shit when its raining like now, or when it's cold, or when he's dying. The rifleman out here has to be in fine physical condition and mental condition too, with an enemy like the one we have, and the civilians all around us. And more than anything else, remember this — wars are won by remnants, remnants of materials, remnants of units, remnants of morale. Victory goes to the side whose remnants hold out the longest, and in this war, like any other war, the Marine Corps will hold out longer than anyone else — and the same is true in pacification. They say we're killers. Well, we're being fathers and brothers out here, if they'll let us."

Then there was a sharp explosion, as another mortar round came in. Our heads shot up listening, and we dove into our holes as we heard the onrush of more shells, deep rasping noises in the rain; and huddled there in the hole, the water cold and an assault to my well-being . . . I felt alone and afraid and I wished that men could be brothers. But I wondered as I felt the metallic rips of shells bursting near me whether it was possible in Vietnam — mortars were definitely the fashion.

✹

When it was over and morning had come and the sun was shining, I felt better. There was an air of normalcy to the bivouac. They had built a small shower, and there was a hot kitchen. They were conducting patrols every day. There was talk of an offensive mounting soon. The days were very hot, and the nights were thunderous with an incessant rain. The camp was a haven of sorts, and after being out on a patrol, the men were glad to get back to it for a shower and a hot meal. And when they weren't fighting, the Marines were trying to make life a little better in the refugee villages. Nowhere in South Vietnam did I see anyone work harder than the U.S. Marines to create a normal life for the people shattered by the war.

✾

There was no rural government to represent Saigon with any force or influence. The real policy of the land was made by the Viet Cong. They collected taxes and they promised redistribution of the land when they won the war. More recently, the Viet Cong had taken harsher measures against the peasantry, forcing young men to join their ranks, arresting and executing Vietnamese who had spoken out against the National Liberation Front. The use of terror by the Viet Cong gave the Marines their opportunity. Peasants who were afraid of the Viet Cong abandoned their land. They came to Vietnamese government refugee camps, located near the Marines. Other peasants quit their ancestral homes and lands because they were afraid of the war. Some of the people were probably Viet Cong spies, but they were the few among many, and there was no positive way to weed the spies out. The Marines felt that protection was better than suspicion. Escalation in the war meant escalation of suffering. For better or worse the Marines decided that the wisest course was to see how they could help the people. The refugee camps were set up by the Saigon government. The Marines were invited to help out, but not to take over. In theory, the Vietnamese camp officials wanted the food the Marines could give, but no more. The Marines had other ideas, and they were based on hard-boiled idealism. They knew that nothing could be done in a hurry and they made the children their target. Short or long war? No one knew, but one thing was certain, the future of Vietnam would be the next generation, and the first thing to annihilate after hunger was illiteracy.

I saw what the Marines meant when I went to a refugee camp on my own. I had an interpreter with me, and as we traveled down the road to the camp, it was lined with scores of unhappy-looking people, many wounded and bloody, many walking with listlessness. Their faces no longer seemed to care. The atmosphere in the camp was marked with the finality of imprisonment. After many talks with them, I learned that they had contempt for the barracks buildings built by the Saigon government with American dollars. They did not like the barbed wire and the Vietnamese guards posted around the camp. They found the location insufferable because it was out in the open and always hot. But some U.S. Embassy AID people who were there were proud of the camp. They said it was a model refugee village, and they took many pictures for the files in Washington. When the Vietnamese refugees received cigarettes, they smiled for the cameras. The AID people were particularly proud of the cement latrines in the camp.

Once the AID people had gone away, the refugees said the cement latrines were a violation of privacy; family life was more important. They deplored the lack of shade and said Vietnamese were unhappy without the green cool shadowed comfort of a traditional village. Beyond this they were uprooted; they could not go back. The damage was permanent. The Saigon government enjoys an unrivaled capacity for describing the human problem solved when a refugee is put into a camp. But the people become something unimportant, and they know this as they wait out the war in uncertainty and misery. To the Marines' credit they realized that the way to attack the present misery was through education of the young people. And in their own quiet way, the Marines put their theory to work, building one-room schoolhouses in the camps, realizing that any teacher was better than none — even if the teacher was sympathetic to the Viet Cong!

✧

The importance of education, and the difficulty an American has in gaining acceptance within the inner circle of the civilians who have suffered from the Vietnam war became clear to me one day in another camp. I noticed that the Vietnamese drew away and talked in tight close conversation. I felt I was excluded. Under the best of circumstances it was difficult to make their acquaintance, and in a refugee camp they wore masks, smiling, or rendering whatever action they felt was expected for the moment, and then withdrawing. On this day, I saw a refugee whose name, I later discovered, is Nguyen Van Lien. When I met him he was thirty-three years old. As I was soon to learn, he came from the North. He caught my attention because he looked different. His skin was dark, and he did not let himself act impressed at the arrival of an American, as did many other refugees, hoping for some kind of handout. But what was even more remarkable was the circle of children around him, sitting on the ground, and not moving to surround the jeep I was driving. Their discipline was extraordinary.

They were part of something outside the camp, something that had unmistakable meaning to them. I saw that he was teaching, and I got out of the jeep and asked my interpreter what it was they were learning. The Vietnamese language, said the interpreter. The dark-skinned teacher, Nguyen, had no paper, no pencils, and so he was scratching out on the white sandy ground the basic alphabet of the Vietnamese language which is in Roman characters — a system that was invented in the 17th century by one of the early French Catholic missionaries, adopted for official purposes by the French in 1910, and carried on to this day. It is an easy language to teach, and Nguyen had the attention of the ragged children listening to his intense voice. I stood there, watching, and his eyes looked up at me very quickly, and I sensed a flash of resentment, as if he did not want me to share in this experience. I knew he wouldn't dare to tell me to go away, and I stayed there even though I sensed I was not wanted. He was very patient with the children and they liked him, and I decided that I would leave the only alive circle in the entire refugee camp. I left with a feeling of vexation that my presence was not wanted, and worse, the distinct impression that my standing there was corrupting them somehow. And then I thought that the wall between us was perhaps unreal, something I had made up, and I decided to go back the next day, bringing some paper and a few pencils. I realized that I was forcing a meeting with the modest gift, and I also knew that Nguyen had a story, and I was curious. There wasn't a single hour in Vietnam when you didn't hear the phrase that this was a double war — a military war to defeat the Viet Cong, and a more subtle war to win the hearts and the minds of the people. I believe in the theory that the mind is everything, and I was making of this encounter with Nguyen a battle of minds. I wasn't trying to conquer him. I wanted to know who he was.

The next day, I found him in the same place, and this time I waited until they were finished. He showed no more welcome than he had the day before. I smiled when they smiled, and laughed when they laughed over some joke that I obviously did not understand. For all I knew, they might well be taking advantage of my ignorance of Vietnamese to make me the subject of their laughter.

When the class was finished, he ordered them away.

"Why do you come here?" he said. I wasn't surprised that he spoke English.

"I brought these," I said, offering my peace token of note paper and pencils. They were wrapped up clumsily in a piece of newspaper. He felt the package and understood what it was without bothering to open the package.

"Thank you," he said, "but I don't need it."

"Why not?"

"Because this way, they won't forget, and they will know that it was a Vietnamese using what he had to teach them the language, and not this —" and so saying, he handed me back the package.

I wouldn't take it, and I told him so. "Use it for yourself," I added.

He smiled at that. "I won't cheat you out of giving a present," he said. "Americans always feel cheated when they give something and don't get something back. What do you want?"

I told him I wanted to talk to him. Did he have anything better to do?

He agreed that he wouldn't mind talking for a bit. I offered him a cigarette, and he took it, and he held it up looking at the label. "Salem," he said. "Prime Minister Ky's favorite brand. He likes these." There was no hiding the sarcasm in his voice.

I lighted our cigarettes and we sat down in a little corner of shade, and I asked him what he had against Premier Ky.

"He's not one of us," he said.

"What do you mean?" I exploded. "He's done some very brave things in his life. He is trying."

"Let me tell you something," he said. "Anyone who is a general in Vietnam tries for himself. For his glory. He works for no one else but himself." His voice was calm and assured. It was irritating to listen to him, talking to me as if I were a child learning the alphabet.

"What are you doing to win this war?" I asked him.

"Nothing to win it," he said. "And everything to end it."

Then I stopped arguing with him, and I listened. Whether it was because he had me there as an audience, or because right then he felt like having his life pass before us, he started talking — and I was getting what I wanted.

He remembered his early boyhood in Hanoi, before there was any war. His school and his family life were the center of his existence. He had two younger brothers and one older sister. I gathered that his father was something of a civil servant under the French, and because he was a non-Catholic, his father never received the promotions or the recognition he should have had. In his home, he first heard about Ho Chi Minh. The windows were closed at night, and the living room was a meeting place where his father and a few other men talked about Ho Chi Minh and how to get rid of the French. Sometimes there were errands to run for his father and the secret group, and Nguyen would deliver notes from one end of Hanoi to the other. He presumed then that his mission was dangerous, but now he realized that he was probably carrying nothing too important. Still he spoke with pride of those early meetings and missions. He was ten years old when the Japanese came, but his schooling continued, and he hoped to be a teacher. He did extremely well on his examinations and he was admitted to the university, but those ambitions were ground up in 1945, when his father took all the children out of school and fled Hanoi to join Ho Chi Minh. Then the regularity of classes and studies was lost. He became a runner for the Viet Minh guerrilla forces. He was brighter than most of the young volunteers like himself. He was happy to sacrifice his education for the life he was leading because his father believed in it and because he was convinced that life in Vietnam would be perpetual injustice with the French ruling the country.

"In those days," he said, "I felt my whole spirit lighted up with a flame. I was working for a free country, a free land. It is a feeling we all had, because there is nothing nobler than to know that what you do is for something bigger than yourself. It involved all the people, and it made us all one family. For instance, a number of us in those days helped to devise the method where the Viet Minh would supply the guerrillas by bicycles. We learned to put enough rice and ammunition on one bicycle so that it carried more than what four men could carry on their backs. And later, the Viet Minh perfected this even more so that when they met the French at Dien Bien Phu, they were able to supply an army of ten thousand men by bicycle. The beginning of every day was sweet then. You stretched and you felt freedom in your body. I guess those were the happiest days of my life. We measured each day as one day closer to freeing Vietnam . . . "

"What happened, how did you get down here?" I asked him. He had stopped talking. His face was a secret, and I reassured him that this conversation was our secret, that I really wanted to know about him, and that I was not a spy.

"If I thought you worked for the C.I.A.," he said, "I would not be talking to you at all."

Hearing him say the C.I.A. so loosely and casually was like hearing something decadent or revered mentioned at the wrong time and place. The C.I.A., however, as I learned soon enough in Vietnam, is something everyone knows about. You cannot get far into a conversation with any Vietnamese, and not hear the C.I.A. mentioned. After a while it becomes amusing, because the tendency among Americans is to keep the C.I.A. faceless, mysterious, and out of our minds, as though it were an act of betrayal to admit that the C.I.A. exists. In Vietnam, the C.I.A. is the mother of all plots and counterplots, and no one knows it better than the Vietnamese themselves. Some welcome the C.I.A. as a shaping force, some ridicule it as shaping the wrong forces, but no one eliminates the C.I.A. whenever a serious discussion is held by Vietnamese about their country. I was happy to reassure Nguyen that I did not work for the C.I.A., and presently he was talking again.

He became a prisoner in January, 1951, when the Viet Minh were defeated by the French in a big battle near Vinh Yen. He had not fought in the actual combat, but after the fighting was over, he and some other young men were sent onto the battlefield as scavengers. He said it was heartbreaking, but it had to be done, going over the bodies of the dead, taking off their ammunition belts and their rifles and their identification papers. They did their work in the hours before dawn when the French were still out of sight. He had to overcome the fear of battlefield silence and he ran from body to body and then he was caught in the red burst of a flare, and he had been warned about this, so he froze. Later, it was dark again, and he and three other boys continued gathering together what could be used again from the dead bodies. And then they were captured. No questions were asked of them. The French paratroopers beat them and tied them up, and they thought they were going to be killed. But they were taken to Haiphong, and then he was sick for a long time and he thought there was a spell when he was insane. He never knew whether it was day or night because the cell he was thrown into had a half dozen other prisoners and no windows. Two Senegalese who had tried to desert were thrown in with them and then shot one morning. He cried when he heard the shots because it felt like himself being shot. He realized again what it meant to have a colonial ruler — even in death, you cannot turn to your own people for mercy.

Before Dien Bien Phu, he was transferred to a rubber plantation near Saigon, where they needed workers. The French manager made him a bookkeeper, and his life became almost normal. He met a girl and he forgot about the North. They got married, she became pregnant, and after his son was born, they lived quietly. They had found a meaning in being together as a family, and when the Geneva Convention gave them the choice of returning to the North, he decided to stay on the rubber plantation. His wife was a southerner. He continued his studies, waiting for the time when there would be elections, certain that Vietnam would be united into one country. Secretly, he wanted a united Vietnam. Openly, he lived a careful sober life, waiting to see what would happen after President Diem came into power. He said that if Diem had not been such a madman it was quite possible that peace would have been realized between North and South Vietnam. But Diem's manipulation of power for himself and his family, his enslaving and trapping of all legitimate political rivals to himself brought on another monstrous period, and the National Liberation Front, the Viet Cong, with all its attendant reaction to Diem, was to be expected and anticipated. His wife and child were killed in a fight between Viet Cong and government troops. He had been away in Saigon, and the Viet Cong had gone into his house looking for medicines when they were trapped by the government troops, and in the ensuing fight, the Diem forces had dropped mortar rounds on his house, and his wife and son had died. After that, he had contempt for everyone and everything. He said he became a companion of refugees fleeing the rubber plantation. He was like them, alone, driven away, his memories of family exploded into pieces of tragedy. He learned to avoid questioning by the national police and getting himself drafted into the army of either the government or the Viet Cong. He wanted no handouts from the Americans. He took no pleasure in anything except the teaching of the language to the children.

As he sat there, the sun now full on his face, he showed no expression, no sorrow, no anger. He said that only the poor people of Vietnam had anything worth saving, that the very rich would leave Vietnam when the Americans left, and the soldiers would quit when there was no more war to fight. He said the poor, the refugees, would have to work to build up any villages left after the war.

Then they could go back to the life they knew, and no matter what the politics of the Vietnam that would result, it would make no difference to the poor, so long as they could work their land and not feel like strangers, as they did now — vagrants, tramps, without the smallest shred of dignity left to them. And he cursed everyone who permitted the war to continue. He said, "Look at the faces of the poor here or in the cities or in the few villages lucky enough to have escaped the war so far, and you will find one common expression of sorrow at how long this goes on. People do not understand this war. People do not care for it."

4. BATTLE

THE ESPRIT that the First Cavalry Division had gained in their stateside maneuvers was not lasting — that kind of esprit can only be earned through battle. The bulk of the division came to Vietnam by sea. Their base camp at An Khe had been secured for them by the irrepressible paratroopers of the 101st Airborne Brigade.

The paratroopers did not cheer the arriving air cavalry men wearing their distinctive yellow and black shield-shaped patch with the horse in the corner. By then, the men of the 101st Airborne felt like veterans, and they were suspicious of the First Cavalry. The Central Highlands were cool at that time of the year, and as the First Cavalry arrived, they in fact transformed the land with their swirling helicopters raising clouds of dust where few men, if any, had ever seen anything like this onslaught. The land had been cleared so that there was room for the "birds" (as the helicopters were called) to settle down on the plateau that soon was to be known as the "golf course," with the ragged Hong Kong mountain looming up in the background. The unconcealed arrival of the Americans was a sharp contrast to the furtive ways of the Viet Cong.

The men of the First Air Cavalry Division were the sexiest outfit in Vietnam, and they knew it. By "sexy" it is meant that they had the excitement, the glamor, the uncertainty of something to be proven and conquered. They came to Vietnam with a bad record behind them in Korea, where the First Cavalry had not distinguished itself. A metamorphosis had taken place in the interval between the Korean War and the Vietnam conflict. Now they were endowed with a new name and a new weapon — they were the Air Cavalry who would use helicopters on a scale never before anticipated in any war at any time. And as the Horse Cavalry of old was supposed to ride hard and charge with abandon, the new helicopter-borne cavalry of the Vietnam war was supposed to achieve surprise by riding into the enemy's midst in helicopters. So the pride the First Cavalry had lost in Korea was revived by its new experimental role as the first division in the United States Army to test out the concept of assault by helicopter. And as the cavalrymen of old were more swashbuckling than the ordinary foot soldier, so the men of the First Air Cavalry came to Vietnam with the attitude that they were special with an advantage over the enemy that no other soldier in Vietnam enjoyed. And this was true. The helicopter had been in use in Vietnam by the American advisers and by the Marines. But everyone had not yet begun to grasp what an enormous potential there was in the helicopter used on a mass scale. The intention of the First Air Cavalry was to put five thousand men into the field by helicopters that would be as integral to the First Cavalry as horses had been to the squadrons of old. The original concept of air mobility through the helicopter had been presented by Lieutenant General James Gavin, one of the army's foremost exponents of airborne warfare. In a country such as Vietnam where the jungle prohibited any comprehensive assault by parachute troops, the helicopter was the alternative, especially against the insurgent warfare in which the Viet Cong had proven themselves past masters. For their debut in Vietnam, the First Air Cavalry had the benefit of one year's training at Fort Benning, Georgia, where in problem after problem, the helicopters had been tested under simulated battle conditions. The Infantry School at Benning had its detractors for the airborne concept. The test of whether or not the United States had found something that could stop the Viet Cong came in the late spring of 1965, when the First Air Cavalry was alerted for Vietnam duty. The place chosen for the First Cavalry was An Khe in the Central Highlands. No place in Vietnam could be more of a challenge than An Khe, the ideal terrain for war such as the First Air Cavalry anticipated. The Central Highlands in a time of peace would be a hunter's paradise. Every kind of big game abounds in the jungle, the rolling hills, and the mountains that stretch along the Cambodian border. It is a vast area of uninhabited timber forest and rushing mountain streams. Few people have ever lived in the Highlands because there are legends of evil spirits and the land itself is so hostile that few would care to fight its loneliness and desolate ruggedness. But for armies it was a perfect landscape.

A troopship brought the First Cavalry ingloriously to Vietnam. They were glad to see the white beaches of Qui Nhon; behind them were the memories of a foul voyage, such as many men had traveled before them in the Second World War. There was no tension to their crossing. They didn't feel that danger was imminent because there was no threat of any enemy submarine torpedoing their troopship. But the conditions on the troopship were appalling. Twenty years after the Second World War nothing had changed: the steel bunks were still in five tiers, the smells were as pungent, the gambling continued, and the holds were packed as tightly as ever — so when they came ashore, they were glad to be in Vietnam. Anything was better than the festering oppression aboard the troopship. When they got to the cool hills of An Khe, with red soil all around, they believed it wouldn't be so bad after all. The village of An Khe was quaint enough, and the bare-breasted Montagnard women, traveling along the side of the road with their burdens balanced on their shoulders, roused a whistle and more. In those first days in Vietnam, everything worked efficiently, so that one of the GI's said, "Gee, if you didn't tell me it was Vietnam, I'd think we were on an exercise in South Carolina."

Then the illusion disappeared when the Special Forces camp at Ple Me came under attack from the Viet Cong. The brunt of the American fighting role in Vietnam until the fall of 1965 was borne by the Special Forces camps, run by the elite Green Beret force, who worshiped President John F. Kennedy for giving them back their role of being the U.S. Army's counterinsurgency experts par excellence. Not only that, he had authorized them to wear the green beret that had been taken away from them by some general who had found them overbearing and had little faith in the notion that a small band of men could provide a link with the people of the land and train them so that they would stand and fight off an enemy. Much of what the Special Forces has done in other parts of the world remains classified. But in Vietnam, their operations were pretty much common knowledge, due in large part to the book called *The Green Berets.*

In October, 1965, when the Green Beret camp at Ple Me had come under attack from a Viet Cong force, some units of the First Air Cavalry were committed to help the Americans defend the camp. The operation had been launched by the Viet Cong who had wanted to overrun and destroy the camp. They were not particularly interested in holding the camp; they wanted to show that they were militarily strong. They had escalated the war in the South, heralding the new phase of their military offensive, and were no longer content to wage guerrilla warfare. The emphasis now was on a political victory that would destroy the governmental systems the United States had supported. They now felt strong enough to destroy the political systems quickly and decisively with military victories. And because the threat of their winning was real, the Americans had decided to commit American troops to the Vietnam war. So now, the exuberant Viet Cong felt complete confidence. One of their orders published at the time stated that victory for the National Liberation Front was visible on the horizon. "Our day of justification has arrived," said the order.

The boast had not been ignored by the Americans. They knew that the North Vietnamese had begun sending troops down from the North to assist the Viet Cong. The estimate at that time was that some 50,000 North Vietnamese regulars were committed to the war in South Vietnam. The North Vietnamese Army has 300,000 fully equipped soldiers, and there are another million and a quarter men in a national guard. The Viet Cong force, which it must be remembered is a South Vietnamese force, numbered about 200,000 armed men.

The basic reason for the arrival of the North Vietnamese was to encourage the Viet Cong. But the North Vietnamese were, in large part, to be additional strength for the Viet Cong. They were aiding them, giving them all the military help they could. So if the Americans were assembling troops to help the South Vietnamese, the North Vietnamese were also assembling troops in the South to aid the Viet Cong. In the present and ever-present whirl of rumor and confusion that is part of the Vietnam war, one fact should be viewed correctly — if you must say that the North Vietnamese have invaded the South, then there is equal validity to the North Vietnamese claim that their action is justified in light of our own presence, a presence they prefer to call invasion by the United States troops. It would seem reasonable that neither side is deserving of the description as invader. Both the North Vietnamese and the Americans are present, participating in an undeclared war, fighting one another, trying to determine which South Vietnamese side will win — the Saigon government as it presently stands or the Viet Cong. It is further true that the war in South Vietnam is a civil war. It must be. There are 275,000 South Vietnamese soldiers facing 200,000 Viet Cong who are not people transplanted from any other part of Asia. The Viet Cong are South Vietnamese. Their revolution began in the South, and they are fighting to win it on the soil of South Vietnam. They were clearly winning it before the Americans arrived. Now, it is the Americans fighting the South Vietnamese — that is, the Viet Cong and the North Vietnamese who have come to the South to help the Viet Cong. In short, there can be no question as to who is doing the fighting. Day after day the battle reports are overwhelmingly descriptions of Americans in combat. Already the Saigon government has announced that in the future Americans will be used exclusively for combat, while the South Vietnamese attempt to fashion some sort of control over the people. Bored with the fighting, or tired of it, or admitting that they cannot win the military war, the Saigon government has set itself the less arduous role of a triumph in the area of loyalty. Their chances of success appear negligible.

The Viet Cong go on fighting. They can rally support for an attack against any American installation. They strike from villages that are within earshot of the American base camps at Pleiku, Bien Hoa, and Saigon itself, not to mention a host of lesser towns and villages where the Americans have had a chance to develop friends — but apparently friends not nearly as loyal to the Americans as to the Viet Cong. Any summary of the war in South Vietnam is neither accurate nor sensible if it ignores the fact that the citizens of South Vietnam are fighting a war among themselves, a civil war, that would long ago have been done and over with if the Americans were not present. And it should be generally conceded that if the South Vietnamese had fought out their own war without Americans involved, the Viet Cong would have won, and the country of South Vietnam today would be joined with the North in a single Communist country that would extend for 1200 miles along the coast of Southeast Asia. That much land is important. It is a toehold in Southeast Asia, and it is for this reason that we are in South Vietnam. I don't think we are going to improve anyone's status in South Vietnam by being there; they can do very well by themselves; but we are maintaining the status of the United States as an Asiatic power by remaining on the soil of South Vietnam. The men of the First Cavalry were motivated by that when they got into the first battle of the Chu Phong–Ia Drang Valley. They said that they were not fighting to end the poverty of the South Vietnamese. They did not care about that. What they did say, however, was that they would rather be fighting in South Vietnam than fighting on the borders of Mexico.

*

The four provinces of the Central Highlands are Kontum, Pleiku, Darlac, and Quang Duc. The targets of the North Vietnamese were Kontum and Pleiku. They could take positions on the Cambodian side of the border, and build up and rest their forces before striking into the Highlands. They had no plan for a frontal assault because this was nearly impenetrable country. Where there were no mountains, there were valleys that were still jungle and plains of high elephant grass. Few, if any, people lived in the border areas. The terrain afforded the enemy everything he felt would work to his advantage — cover from the American aircraft, food and water, and most of all, the kind of country that he had gotten used to on his march down from the North along what the newspapers had come to call the Ho Chi Minh trail. This is not one single route, but a maze of intertwining trails that are barely wide enough for one man at a time.

If you are to imagine the Ho Chi Minh trail, do not think of it as a wide passage with clear measured distances, do not think of anything modern. Think of the thickest forest you have ever seen, where there are no markers, no blazes in the trees. Think of dense passageways where strength is needed to see and to walk. Think of the effort it takes for one man carrying all his personal gear and his weapon and ammunition to march at the rate of thirty kilometers a day with one ration of rice, and you have some idea of what the enemy is. He is subject to bombing if he is ever spotted, which is rare (despite the American bombing, 8,000 men a month march to the South from the North). He is more vulnerable to disease, especially to the malaria he will almost surely encounter on the sixty-day march from North Vietnam to the Central Highlands of South Vietnam. He has no medical evacuation. He has been uprooted from his home. But he does not think the war is useless or in vain.

✽

The First Cavalry came into the Ia Drang Valley, north of the Chu Phong Mountain, by helicopter. The landing zone was called X-ray, and as the helicopters swept down toward the area, the pilots of the 229th Lift Company thought it looked like peaceful country. They were close to the enemy when they landed but there was nothing to tell them that. They hopped out of the choppers and they spread out; the choppers bobbed and then, as if relieved that they were still able to fly, gave a sudden burst of speed and were up in the air and away. Soon the men on the ground were aware of only one thing — silence, the dread silence of knowing that the choppers were gone and they were now on their own. A helicopter assault is like any other kind of assault, tense, "hairy" the men in Vietnam call it, and there is always the fear as you come in for the assault that the enemy will be ready down below and will shoot up the choppers and the men in them, and there will be nothing to stop the men from dying. Anyone who has ever been afraid recognizes that fear sounds are in him, heard by him, and therefore he assumes heard by everyone else. But fear sounds, no matter how loud they seem to the man who knows they are his, are drowned out by the racket the choppers make. As soon as the choppers have left, sound leaves too. The towering sense of communication with the outside is gone. Now, the men of the First Battalion, 7th Cavalry were on their own. Their commander, Hal Moore, 44 years old, of Bardstown, Kentucky, smelled the air and it reminded him of North Carolina and the maneuvers the First Cavalry had conducted there. He could see the mountain ahead, and the thick forest on the slopes was like Carolina, too. Moore is a West Pointer and a professional soldier who had waited for this, his first combat assignment. He had been to many schools, the Armed Forces Staff College, the U.S. Naval War College, the Infantry School, the Command and General Staff College. He had his Master's Degree in International Affairs from George Washington University. But all of the degrees and the classes were only preparation of a kind for this, his moment of truth. His boyhood had been spent in woodlands, and he was the kind of man who felt at home in places where earth and branches and light, and sound, too, are all calculations in the hunter's mind as he stalks whatever it is that he is hunting. Now, all the terms of battle order and the slide rules and coffee breaks, the notebooks, and the instructors of all those colleges and universities were far less important than how Colonel Moore and his men would react when they met the enemy. That was something you could not be taught. You either had it, or you did not. None of these things were consciously in their minds as they proceeded toward the mountain, but still, they were men composed of all their experiences, and the curtain that would protect them or defeat them was nothing fabricated. It was genuine. There are no private lives in combat. Everyone is identical. A target. All the credentials of private life are of no value in combat. The only charm that would protect a man from dying was his luck, or his ability to react fast enough, or even his ability to understand solitude.

They had crossed the valley and were at the foot of the mountain when the solitude was broken, when they became targets. The official description is that they came under intensive fire from the hill mass ahead.

Actually, each man had become a target. The enemy on the slopes of the Chu Phong were North Vietnamese. They had watched the Americans cross the valley, and they had waited for them to get less intense and less alert than they were when they landed. The enemy was also smart enough to know that if they waited long enough the choppers would be far enough away for them to massacre the Americans before the choppers could come back and help. The enemy did not know as much about choppers then, that November day in 1965, as they were to know later about how vulnerable they were to ground fire. So they had watched the Americans come closer, and then when they were well within range of their guns, the North Vietnamese let loose. The enemy rose up, showed himself, and charged toward the Americans on the lower slopes of the Chu Phong Mountain.

*

The men, seeing the enemy appear like that, standing and charging forward, were openmouthed, and many of them later were to remember that they thought they were watching something on television. They did not believe that it was going to be like this, and what made them come to, become participants again in the battle, was the deadly realization that all around them were the fragments of mortars and the sound of more gunfire and the terrible smell of a battle. The North Vietnamese kept coming down the hill, and the Americans wondered why they were not all dead. The American artillery shells were now landing up there, and the First Cavalry did not even think about the artillery as helping them because the shells were falling so close. They could not hear them going over, but they were landing close, and much of the shrapnel was falling near them, and the concussion was something they felt as their sweat ran free. They prayed that the American artillerymen did not make a mistake, even a small one, because then they would not stand a chance. Later, reminiscing about it, one of them, a Negro corporal, would say, "You know, it was funny out there, in the middle of it all, I didn't blame anyone for my being there. I just wanted it to be over and me out of it safe, and I promised God, and I'm not the prayin' kind, that I would be thankful. I am thankful. I mean I don't hate anyone, anymore."

❋

All the foliage splintered around him was the way another of the troopers remembered it afterwards. The din of the fire was vicious and constant, and he knew right there and then that this was solitude of the most painful kind, hugging the ground, twisting and digging with his body to disappear down into the ground. The men around him were doing the same, yet some were firing back, and he wondered how they could fire when all he wanted to do was get beneath the surface of the earth, away from the zinging tearing sound of the invisible buzz saws ripping and tearing branches, splintering and bursting the day into unaccustomed questions that he had no time or inclination to answer. He saw one of his buddies hit, and the impact of the bullets — he saw that it was not a single round but a fusillade — turned the body over and over, as if it were an object, not a man, being pushed around by an army of invisible midgets. Then he began firing back. He didn't know it then, but his platoon was isolated from the rest of the battalion. They were to be that way for seventy-two hours.

❋

At the first sign of contact, Colonel Moore got on the radio. He called for air strikes and artillery to hit the side of the mountain. He ordered his men to hold their positions.

The battle broke up into many pieces. Anyone trying to recreate it afterwards would feel that the happenings of those seventy-two hours were not one picture, but many, all with ragged edges. One of the commanders was to say that it was strangely like city fighting or what he thought city fighting was like — combat at every corner, the enemy likely to be in any of the windows around you, each block becoming its own battleground. Another said it was like prospecting for oil — you went out and you hit a gusher; it spilled hell and death all over everyone.

*

I saw the first battle of the Ia Drang Valley in its closing hours. I had left Saigon early in the morning, hitching a ride on a C-123. With me were my crew, cameraman Vo Huyhn, and a sound man named Giac. Vo Huyhn was unlike any other Vietnamese I had ever met. He had come down from North Vietnam and his eyes were the first thing you ever noticed about him. They seemed to have imprisoned in them calm or suspicion or knowledge, or a combination of all three. He had seen many combat situations in South Vietnam and he was one of the best cameramen to be found anywhere in Asia. He was not one for horseplay or jokes. He was serious about gambling, and about his camera work, and about fighting. Part of the lore that had built up around him was that in one situation when a Vietnamese company was in danger of being overrun he had taken over from the commander and outwitted the enemy, holding the position against what seemed to be certain annihilation. In this fight, it was said, he had crawled out ahead of his own lines to take ammunition from the bodies of the dead enemy and friendly soldiers. Certainly in his face now as we flew north toward what was the biggest battle of the war, there was no sign that he would flinch from any danger we might be asked to face.

We landed at Pleiku and from there we hitched a ride on a chopper going down to the forward command post. By now, a brigade had been committed to the battle, and the man in charge was Brigadier General Richard Knowles, a tall Georgian who said he was going down into the combat area and that he had room for two of us if we wanted to go along. This meant that we would drop our sound man, so only Vo Huyhn and I were to go. We shared the load of the equipment that we were going to take in with us. The general warned us that once we got in we would be on our own. There was no way of telling when we would get out, but I expected that, and told him as much.

We ran into trouble as we first approached the landing zone named X-ray. Fighting was still going on on the ground, and our people down there were warning us off. I had the *cans*, the earphones, over my ears and I could hear them pleading that we not come any closer.

As soon as they told us that we could come in, the chopper brought us down very low, flitting right over the treetops. The scene below was chilling. There were bodies on the ground, and you knew which were the dead because they were all in one silent pile at one side of the landing zone. Seeing them like that — detached, lifeless — was enough to give me the idea that looking on death was something contagious. I looked away and I could see where the mortar crews were still firing.

A battleground is like handwriting when you see it from the air, a careless signature that has been written across the ground. The sight of the men down there filled me with hope that if they had survived, we would, too.

When we got down to the strip, everybody crowded around and some officer was yelling, desperate, and yet unheard and unlistened to. There wasn't a happy face any-where. The men stumbled more than they walked. They said they needed water and food. Everything had been stripped from their faces except the emotion of surprise — they were living. There were whispers among them about who needed to go first.

Staring, confused by all the noise of mortar and artillery landing nearby, I climbed off the chopper with Vo Huyhn. Some of the men looked at Vo suspiciously. He was the only Vietnamese there, and the only faces like his they had seen belonged to the enemy. So they were suspicious of him. I explained that he was working for NBC and he was with me. He had great dignity in his face and in his bearing and that, too, helped kill any of their suspicions.

"You think he's a spy," said a soldier with a three-days' growth of beard and eyes so red they looked as though he had been on a week-long drunk without any sleep. Soldier's eyes, I thought, with the blur of battle and the heartbreak of life and death blazing red from them.

We walked away from the crowd around the general who had said he had run the battle like a management team. There was no computer efficiency on the battlefield. The quiet glen had been disfigured by men fighting for their lives. Tree after tree was splintered by the intense fire. The ground was chopped and gutted as if a madman had been on the rampage with a chain saw. There were now two piles of dead soldiers, and whoever had piled them up had done so with a sense of military discipline because all their feet were lined up. That was all that showed — the soles of their boots in a perfect line, as if the dead were on review. In one line were six pairs of shoes, in the other about twice as many. They were covered by rain ponchos, and near them were piles of helmets and webbing and packs the men no longer needed. Here the efficiency of computer warfare was evident. Somehow, someone was responsible for accumulating the dead soldiers' equipment so it would not be left on the battlefield. But there were other signs of less intense discipline — the pieces of C–rations, paper cartons lying around in a litter, and above it all, there was the choking sense of dust and smoke and uncertainty. It was too cold to smell death. All around were the men who had survived, crouched in their foxholes, a diversity of men who all looked alike now, no change in their faces, all besmeared with dirt and fatigue and danger. And the memory of what they had lived through was part of the similar expression they all wore. More mortar explosions came in very loud and very near and the men reacted as one, disappearing down into their holes and their return fire going out into the tree line, unseen fire, but bringing with it the sound of someone screaming, a human sound louder and more penetrating than the ground fire. Then the flag.

It was the only color anywhere. The men's fatigue uniforms had taken on the color of the earth, and the men themselves were all of an earthen color. Even their helmets had blended into a monochrome that was constant. But the flag was something else. It was tiny, the kind of flag sold to children for Fourth of July celebrations, and it hung from the branches of a bullet-splintered tree. The men below it were glad that it was there. I realized then what their patriotism was, and it was formidable. Three days ago they had not been in combat, and now all the memories of combat were theirs, and whatever they would remember about the Ia Drang would include the flag. No one had engineered the flag's being there. It had not been part of the standard equipment that went into combat with them. But one of them had cared enough to carry it and display it this way. And the flag was like a chain between them, a sort of megaphone that shouted out that they had been there, a new generation of Americans who were bound to others before them by the flag. The meaning of the flag was unlimited. Not one of the troopers pointed it out to me, no one yelled and shouted that I film it for the television audience back in the States. But the fact that it was there was something that could not be denied, or ignored, or forgotten.

I went and asked the men in the hole beneath it, who had put it up. A soldier who had a blood-soaked bandage around his upper arm where the sleeve had been cut off so that the wound could be looked after, said, "He's over there, now." And his face looked to the pile of the dead. It was a moment of intolerable pain to see the look he gave the pile. Then he looked back at me, and he said, "He bought the flag in Times Square when he was up there on furlough. I've never been up there myself, but he said he had a good time. He also got himself a flag tattoo. Had it right up here," and he indicated his wound, "only on him it looked kind of funny because he hadn't many muscles. His arms was real skinny."

Then they set to work digging their holes deeper. As they worked we filmed them, and in the queer early morning light, with the gunfire around us, it seemed like a scene where they were gravediggers — that was the feeling they gave. It seemed almost too cruel that men dug holes in the ground to stay alive.

All of a sudden a tremendous racket of incoming fire swept over landing zone X-ray, and all the motion stopped as men everywhere hit the ground. I found myself next to a young soldier who looked very tired. He was looking ahead to the tree line where we could sense the enemy were, firing into the landing zone. The general's choppers had already taken off, and there was nothing on the landing zone now but us. I asked him what he thought was happening, and he said he didn't know. We lay with our bodies hugging the ground and our faces down, looking out straight ahead, but the sound of our voices was distinct enough to us. I often wondered how it was that men under fire could hear one another, and I felt that maybe it was because our mouths were pressed into the ground and the voices carried under the ground to our ears, pressed down into the earth. Maybe that, or maybe just that it was reassuring to be able to hear one human sound above all that raging uncontrollable sound of gunfire that has no distinct voice. It has been described by some as having a specific character, but every time I have heard it, all I can think of is something sticky and menacing. I can't honestly say that I remember it as a mournful cry or anything that I can name as something distinguishable. And as quickly as it had come, it had died down. The officers and the non-coms were shouting that it was just a sniper and they had got him and for everyone to stop firing. *Pass the word along, pass the word along*, was now a loud sound of relief that it was over.

I marched over to where Colonel Hal Moore was hunched over his map. He was young-looking, and he described some of the fighting, and his voice was choked and tears were in his eyes. "I don't know what they're saying in Berkeley or any other place back home, but I just want to tell you that these are the bravest men any country ever had. You know the enemy, he was attacking us. He was coming down the mountain after us. And I can tell you that we didn't do the attacking. We just made the contact and then we settled down into our positions and we fought him back. Human life is the enemy's cheapest commodity. He can afford to lose ten men to every one of ours.

We were sent in here, looking for him, not to take any real estate. They were surprised to find us here. They decided to test us out. They're trained. They're professionals. They hurt us. I admit that. But they didn't lick us. This was man-to-man fighting, a free-for-all like they can never describe in the textbooks. And you can't say this one is over. Not by a long shot. You know I had a platoon out there, B company, and they were surrounded. They ran out of everything — dexedrine, morphine, bandages, and they were running down to their last rounds of ammunition — and all the time they were talking to me, and they never once said anything about quitting. They just stayed up there. They heard them so close they could smell them. They even heard the bugles they use in the charge, and you know they came out of that fight with the bugle. You go on over and talk to them and you'll see what I mean, because they are the bravest there ever was, and you gotta talk to them to understand what I mean."

I went and found them.

"Just kept firing didya?" said a man with a New York Brooklynese accent.

I just came in and sat with them, and they didn't even look up. They just kept talking. It wasn't in me to ask them anything. I was the fly on the wall, listening. And listening was like taking peel after peel off them, peel after peel of what had been sealed up and was now coming off in its own natural way.

"Yeah, I just figured that if I ran outa ammo, I'd stay there and I'd pretend I was dead."

"Go ahead, what then, what happened when you did run out of ammo?"

"I did like I said; I pretended I was dead. They come up and they poked around me, and I remembered everything I could remember about being stiff and not breathin', and they rolled me over. They stink like hell you know. It's not just from not washin'. It's a stinking lousy fish smell, like a whorehouse smell when there's a lot of come all caked all over everything. Dry fish smell, you know. And there was a guy I didn't see, but he was scared, and he had some kind of whoreass powder or talcum like lilacs, and he stank at that. And then when the artillery started comin', this guy he rolled me over and he used me for protection. I mean he was right there lyin' on top of me, and he was using my fucking sweet body as his motherfuckin' sandbag or something . . ."

"Jesus Christ, you mean he was lyin' right there on top of you?"

"Yeah, you bet your sweet ass. He right on top of me figurin' that my sweet ass would stop a few bullets or a chunk of shrapnel."

"Well, weren't you scared?"

"Was I scared? You bet your sweet ass, I was tricklin' shit right out of my asshole, and it was wet and sticky and I was shakin', I mean the way I shook, I couldn't control it or anythin', but I was shakin' and I figured that I was going to get it full in the ass or something from him because I was shakin' so, but you know then it hit me that I was all right."

"What did you mean, all right, with him a-laying atop you? What the fuck do you mean?"

"I mean that was what made it so cute. He was shakin', too, and in all my life I never felt so pussy-good as to hear and feel him shakin', and feel him firing away right atop me, as you say, and I knew then, that if he was a-shaking so almighty bad like that, then he was scared as I was."

They all whistled, hearing that, their faces transfixed in their own reveries of the battle. They all saw themselves in one position or the other. They were compressing the battle into lessons. They were absorbing it, saving it. No rage. Listening to the miracle that had saved one of them, preserving it for the next time.

"How long did he stay on you like that? How long?"

"I can't tell. I can tell you this though. They say a lot of things move through your mind, that you see everything when you think you're dying, like a drowning man seeing his whole lifetime go by in a flash just afore he sinks down — well, that didn't happen to me. All I recall is the stink of that guy. Him shakin'. Me shakin'. I didn't have no memories. I didn't make any promises to God. I tell you I didn't even think of prayin' because I knew that if I did anything but playact dead, he woulda known and that woulda finished me for sure. So I just lay there actin' dead, and trying to keep my shakin' in time with his, just so he's got accustomed to us both shakin' like it were all him, and me just something dead that he had forgot all about."

Now they stared at him.

He stared back into that other time. I calculated it had all happened less than twenty-four hours before, maybe last night. I wanted to ask questions, but it was like listening to a Serkin play the piano. You listen. You think. You feel. But you don't interrupt.

"But it was dark, right?"

"Man, it was dark. My eyes were shut. I just stayed there, and I had my eyes closed and it was dark. I tell you I should get the Oscar for that playactin'. I thought I was dead. I mean I really played it so well. I believed it."

"Then how did he go?"

"I don't know. I just waked up from my actin' and I still was shakin' and he weren't atop me anymore, and it was quiet, and there was no shootin', and I opened my eyes. I saw these red ants goin' acrost my hands, bitin' a bit as they crawled around, and I tell you that was the best feelin' I will ever know, those ants, biting and scratching, and you can think of the best fuck you ever had in your life, and it will never be as good as it was to have those pretty lovely ants just bitin' me, and I feelin' it, and I knew then that I was alive, and where he had gone, I didn't care. I knew that I was livin' and pissed myself I was so happy. I could still smell him where he'd been layin' on me, the lilac fish smell, and I didn't know whether I'd been there a week or one night, but I crawled back to my hole and seen where Tommy was still there, deader'n hell, and they had taken his weapon, and they had taken mine, too, and I figured that I'd get back down the hill to where I figured the CP was, and so I started moving back and that's when I run into the two-five and they sure looked swell. I screamed when I saw them and heard them talkin' American, and I pissed myself again I was so happy . . ."

His voice was exultant. That had been his war, his battle of the Ia Drang Valley. He had gone over it, in his way, in his language, and he told it how he felt it. As he talked, they had been involved in it with him. It wasn't sacrifices they were interested in. They didn't care about the body count of the enemy dead. The knowledge they wanted was how to survive. The news of who was dead they accepted quietly, and that was the limit of their discussion concerning their buddies who had been lost. They retreated from talk about death.

Later, at the Battalion CP, Colonel Moore told me that a B–52 strike was coming in, and that put everyone in high spirits. The B–52's were reserved for the most important targets, and it was the equivalent of making page one to have the B–52's bomb targets you were involved with. Everyone was keyed up for it like a first-night audience that thinks it will be witnessing a hit play. There was also the sense of the other world coming into their battlefield, caring enough to cast their lots in with them. There was no concern that the B–52's would make a mistake. The men believed in the efficiency and the accuracy of the giant aircraft.

"Get out the smoke!" yelled a sergeant, and the men started putting out smoke to mark our lines. Voices screamed "Get 'im!" at the light airplane up in the sky above us; they kept yelling with the joy of hearing their own voices. The B–52's had gotten the exact information long ago, but the light plane was up there, and he was a regular, part of the business of close air support for the infantrymen — the *fac,* for *forward air control.* The pilot of the *fac* had apparently caught some of the excitement because he kept flying, diving down low, buzzing, and wagging his wings.

After a while the GI's got tired and ignored him. They were sitting in their holes, waiting to see what would happen to the mountain ahead where the enemy was located when the B–52's got through bombing it. Their faces were all turned toward the mountain, and they all had on their helmets. Their attentive looks reminded me of people in church, waiting for something, a favorite hymn, or the divine spark to hit them. The fighter planes were working over the Chu Phong flying low, hitting fairly high up, and the landing zone was alive with the concussion and the sound of the bombing by the fighters.

"Them fighters. That's just a warm-up," said a soldier near me.

I asked him if he had ever seen a B–52 strike, and he answered, "Never. I'm burning up to see it. I wonder if there's going to be anything left of that mountain when they get through."

I looked up at the cloudy sky. We wouldn't be able to see the B–52's because they would be up so high. For a moment, it was almost as if we were not in a battle but at a football game, waiting for the kickoff. The Chu Phong was covered with smoke, and you could see that some of the forest was burning. The fighters had gone away, and I wondered what it was like for the enemy up there. The flames kept licking up out of the green, and they looked hot and fierce. Then some more mortar rounds came landing into X-ray, and we flung ourselves down on the ground. They are not dead up there, I thought.

The mortar shells had come close and I could hear one of our boys screaming. I wondered how the enemy could react so fast after the pasting they had taken from the fighters. Somewhere out by the tree line, there was the steady sound of two machine guns firing away. I began to worry if the enemy were closing in for another attack. For all I knew, they weren't up on the mountain at all but around us here on the valley floor. Neil Sheehan of the New York *Times* was near me and he grinned and said, "This place certainly gets spooky."

Colonel Moore was talking into the telephone and there was a sadness on his face. He put the instrument up, and he said, "They're not coming."

"No B–52's?" I said.

"Nope," he said. "They're not coming now. Maybe later. But for now, it's called off."

"What's the matter?" I said. "Why don't they come? The enemy is still out there, isn't he?"

I listened for the machine-gun fire, but it had grown silent, too.

"Well," he said, looking up at the still-burning jungle, "they may be up there, or they may have gone across the border into Cambodia. We're going to be pulled out; there are a lot of choppers coming to take us. A new battalion, McDay's, is coming in."

He motioned toward his men. "They've been fighting for seventy-two hours, and I think it's time they got out."

The helicopters came in quickly, and the men wasted no time getting on them. They ran as fast as they could, without any sense of shame, to get on the choppers and fly out of Landing Zone X-ray. They had forgotten about the B–52 strike they did not see. The choppers were their salvation. Before they climbed out of their holes, they sprayed the foliage ahead of them with their guns. I asked Colonel Moore what they were doing, and he said, "Just like a good-bye kiss. They spray out there, and if there are any of the enemy trying to infiltrate, they'll get discouraged. We did it this morning, and we discouraged them then."

"What is the good of doing it now?" I said.

"It can't do any harm. It's just ammo, and it makes the man feel better. Lets off steam. He clears his weapon now. He's going out, and it gives the fellows coming in a break just in case there is anyone out there."

"The fellows coming in" were five hundred men, the First Battalion of the 5th Cavalry. They moved across Landing Zone X-ray, and out toward the Chu Phong, marching in a northwesterly direction. They were fresh troops, and they looked it. They marched in two lines, and as they faded into the jungle, I wondered if Vo Huyhn and I should go with them. Their orders were to make reconnaissance of the mountain. The feeling was that they would not get into any contact with the enemy. As they went by, I saw how young their faces were, and how they lacked the battle-tiredness in their walk and their carriage that was so evident in Colonel Hal Moore's men. There was no exchange between the soldiers going out and the ones marching into the jungle.

Moore's dead and wounded had already been lifted out so there was no sign of what inferno battle is to depress the men going into the jungle. I felt my nerves on edge at the thought of going along with them. It meant a long hard march and spending the night on the mountain. The discussion as to whether I should go was held entirely with myself, and finally I decided that we already had a story and that had to be sent down to Saigon for shipment to New York. More than that, I felt something scary about the new men, some premonition that they were going to get into trouble. And they did. That afternoon they were caught in a dreadful ambush where many were killed. Deciding not to go was the difference between the men who are correspondents and the men who are doing the fighting. Whether out of weakness or authentic clairvoyance, when a fighting man senses danger, he must follow orders and keep going. The correspondent can leave and that's what I did. From Landing Zone X-ray we were heli-lifted into another safer landing zone, where we were to wait for big Chinook choppers to come in and lift us out to Pleiku where there would be hot showers and food. And that had a strange impact; one landing zone tense and subdivided by foxholes and fields of fires, and the other, less than twenty minutes away, peaceful, where the men lay down exhausted and fell asleep.

Here, the air was clean of battle. There was time to wonder. The GI's simply fell on the ground, no deception now, no digging of holes. Their faces began to change, too. They looked whatever their age was, and they didn't all have the same battered efficiency that stuck to them on X-ray. They were finding themselves again. They were outside of danger now and so they had time to think of themselves, and the missing.

"Have you seen Clyde?"

"No."

"Last I saw of him we were in that fire fight by the creek."

"He was in the KIA bunch. I saw him there."

"Yeah?" The voice was indifferent.

"I'm sure it was Clyde. He was lying next to the kid who just joined up with us before we shipped. The one who snored so bad and lost all that money in the poker game when we were coming over here."

"Could you let me have a cigarette?"

The package of cigarettes was passed around.

They were talking in whispers, not that they didn't want to be heard. It was just the mood, the hangover from the battle.

There were birds somewhere up in the trees, and they were flying around, and the sound of them beat down like summer. Every so often another chopper would bring in more of the men and they would become part of the battalion lying on the ground. The men were separating now, back into their own units, their own platoons. You could feel their mood in the way they lay around, a mood where pain and danger were no longer imminent, and they could lie on their backs and find that the most important pleasure on the earth. Occasionally there was the clink of a canteen as it was passed around and the men drank from it quietly until the last drop was gone, and the GI waved it around, showing that it was empty. Then he sank back to the ground.

I sensed that this moment was terribly important. All the times somewhere else that they would lie on the ground, making love, sharing a picnic, digging a garden, hunting, waiting for the Fourth of July fireworks, resting somewhere else in some other time — all those times to come would never match this moment, because right now they were realizing freedom. Because right now they loved this life, and they were free of the battle that had diminished in the distance. There was no grief for the dead. They were quite at ease with themselves, with their luck, and while it might not last through the next battle, whenever that would be, right now they were content to lie there and listen to the comings and the goings of the helicopters. This time was their own.

Hal Moore was the last man to come out of the battle. It was the biggest battle he had ever fought. He was a lieutenant colonel, and he carried himself like a proud man. His sergeant major was at his side. I love them, Colonel Moore thought. I love them. It would need a Shakespeare to describe just what happened then, but it was something that *was* love and manliness and pride. It was the moment of the brave. Hal Moore turned and went from group to group of his men, and only a few bothered to get up because there was no exclusivity now, no rank, and Hal Moore did not want them to stand and salute. He was saluting them. He talked with them. He thanked them. He was not solemn, and he did not bring to his greetings the salutations of a politician. There was no poverty of spirit in his handshake, and he shook every man's hand. It was a union of the men who had met and defeated the enemy, not forever, not in a victory that ended the war, but in a victory over their own uncertainty. When their hour had come, they had done their job, and it was this thought, too, that Hal Moore had in his mind. And he said that if they had won no one else's gratitude, they had his.

If you feel a protest in your heart reading this, if you really feel that what happened in the Ia Drang Valley was a waste of this nation's talent, that is your opinion. But whenever I have reason to doubt our policy in Vietnam, and I do often enough, I think of the way those men were. Those who do not do battle for their country, do not know with what ease they accept their citizenship in America. The men who do battle in Vietnam wearing the American uniform are undergoing the dirtiest least-honored war this country has ever fought. In many respects, they do not have the reward of their adversaries. The Viet Cong feel that they are defending the soil of their native land, and the American soldier is fighting on a foreign soil. But the American is no less brave; and more so than at any other time in this nation's history, he goes into battle with a dreadful sense of aloneness. For although he has a maximum of supplies behind him and he has the President of the United States honoring the difficulties of Vietnam combat, the GI in Vietnam makes his sacrifice experiencing melancholy. He feels not only the physical distance between himself and home, but the spiritual distance between what he is doing and what his fellow Americans feel about it. Therefore, the GI is all the more admirable, in my opinion, for he has neither honor nor praise to be gained for fighting in Vietnam. He is very much alone, and only those closest to him realize what he is doing. Vietnam is a new school of patriotism. It is hours of dreadful trial for the individual soldier. The people back home, the policy-makers in Washington, should recognize that it is part of the greatness of this country that she provides such men. Is the nation injuring the men, or venerating them?

But at that point, Hal Moore and his men weren't thinking any of these things. They were happy to be out of the Ia Drang Valley alive.

By late afternoon, they were all back at Pleiku. They walked off the big Chinooks and without anyone giving them a command, they straightened up. They were not dirty tired infantrymen any more. Hal Moore's battalion voluntarily dressed their lines, as if they were coming back to life. And the GI's who had not been in the Ia Drang glanced at them with something approaching awe because these were the guys who had been in it. No cheers. But they could not conceal their admiration. A few GI's were taking pictures as we went by — there was something dramatic in the scene all right, because Hal Moore's men had not yet thrown off what they had been through. There was no shouting, no telling off the ones who had been lucky enough to stay back because that was the luck of the draw. But the signal had passed through these men that they were coming back to base camp and they just couldn't march in as if nothing had happened because a great deal had. They marched jauntily and smartly, without making it a production. You would have too, if you had been one of them. The GI's with the clean faces and uniforms watched them to see what they could tell about combat from these men. It was the kind of scene that Hollywood could never produce, because the men had the dirt and gore of combat completely drenched into them. You can only get that dirty and that proud if you have been in combat and survived it. You can't put it on.

They were the center of attention, briefly, and they were enjoying it. They weren't reveling in it, but as one of the GI's said, turning back to look at me, "Lord, it sure feels awful going out there, but there's nothing like getting back."

One base GI pointed his camera at me, and I guess I looked tired, but I realized that I wasn't one of them, not then. I had not done what they had done. And I said to the GI pointing the camera at me, "Don't take my picture. Take theirs. They are the ones that matter." He peered at me as if I were mad. "Hey," he said, "you okay?" There was concern in his voice, yet I didn't bother to answer.

Then the order was given to fall out, and it felt as though an invisible cord that had bound us all into one were cut away, and we were now free to go toward the showers or the chow line or the PX where they had promised beer. The place that everyone headed for first was the PX with its beer.

We clustered around the small counter they had set up inside the tent, and in the first taste of beer, there was the taste of deliverance.

"Well," said the man standing next to me, "this is living."

And someone else picked up the last word, and then they were chanting, "Living . . . yeah, that's what it is . . . living."

They were not drinking down any sorrows. They were embracing one another.

All except one.

There were tears in his eyes. He made his way out of the embracing mass like someone walking in darkness. He stumbled out of the PX tent, still holding his beer as if it were light, guiding him. In the look on his face, the look of a person who has forgotten something. Outside the tent, he took another gulp from the beer can. He set it down next to him. He fumbled around his throat, and he came out with dog tags, and tangled around the string of the dog tags was a rosary and a crucifix. He moved them around his fingers gently, not thinking, not looking, just feeling.

He found the tiny crucifix in the rosary, and he peered at it, raising it to his eyes. The beads and the crucifix blended into his face.

I sat next to him.

"How you doing?" I said.

"What you say?" he said.

His fist closed tight on the beads, on the crucifix.

"How you doing?" I repeated.

He opened his clenched fist.

"Do you see it?" he said.

He peered into the palm of his hand where the crucifix rested.

"What?" I said.

"You see it, don't you? The cross?"

I looked into his palm and saw the cross there. It was a little cross, but it seemed riveted into his own palm.

"I see," I said.

"No you don't."

"Why don't you just say what's on your mind," I said.

"It saved my life," he said.

"What do you mean?"

"It preys on me," he said, "that it really saved my life. I didn't believe it would. But my sister, she believes, and she gave it to me, and she said it would."

He indicated the cross by bouncing it now so that it leaped up and down on his palm.

"Just look at it," he said. "She gave it to me and I took it 'cause in my own mind I knew that if I didn't take it, I'd jinx myself. But I didn't believe it would do me any good. It mattered to her." Then he put the cross and the beads and the dog tags back inside his shirt.

"What happened?" I said.

"I was out there," he said, "and I'm just a guy serving out his time in this army and when we were out there, I thought I'd bought it. I mean I wouldn't of given me a chance. Because I was cut off."

He touched the now hidden dog tags, crucifix, and rosary.

"I was left alone," he continued, "my buddy had been killed, and then this VC he come up at me and he was going to kill me. I know that, and I saw him raise his rifle to zap me for good. I saw it in his eyes. I put my hands inside my shirt and I come out with the cross and I just showed it to him, just the way you would show a state policeman your license. And he looked at me and he looked at the cross and he went on as if I were not there at all. I just don't understand. Do you? I just don't understand unless he was a Catholic."

"Sure," I said. "That's what he was, a Catholic."

"I guess . . . God is on both sides in this war," he said.

5. BROTHERS IN ARMS

THE SUCCESSIVE BLOWS registered by the Americans against the Viet Cong and the North Vietnamese units in South Vietnam had by the arrival of 1967 created a cautious sense of optimism. But American casualities were rising higher week after week; they had gone from an average of 300 to 400 killed and wounded in the fall and winter of 1965 up to 800 and 900 a week in the latter part of 1966. The war itself was governed by some curious rules.

Gigantic military preparations involved thousands of men; but in fact, the operations were limited. There was also the disturbing element that many operations bore an ominous resemblance to the kind that the French had run during their ill-fated presence in Vietnam. The word *operation* itself fitted a limited prescription; basically it meant launching a large force of men, from two to tens of thousands of Americans, sometimes supported by Vietnamese and sometimes not, into an area where the Viet Cong were suspected of living and training. There was something electric about the launching of these operations by helicopter into vast tracts of enemy-controlled areas. The operations began with a powerful demonstration of American airpower and logistical planning; among the details Americans would take into account were such things as the delivery of beer and fresh hot food to the men.

But the people in the cities were not conscious of the war. There was the spectacle of an American billet like the Metropole being blown up, and for a day or so, the headlines in the local Vietnamese papers would admit the presence of the Viet Cong in the cities. Many of the Vietnamese responded to the Viet Cong raids with a certain degree of appreciation. They liked the daring that would destroy one of the American living quarters. Strains were beginning to creep into Vietnamese-American relations. "Your people are too arrogant. You can never imagine how insulted we are by your presence." For the truth of the matter was that there was no escaping the fact that the Americans with their higher pay would come into Saigon on leave, and they would provoke resentment as they hit the bars and began to get the girls, of which there were many available. The contact of Americans with the Vietnamese in Saigon became more tense. The Americans lived in a different world. Their imprint was the money they spent and the barricades they built around their buildings to keep the Vietnamese at a distance. In spite of what was supposed to be a joint effort toward winning the war, there was much that divided and separated the Americans from the Vietnamese. The original purpose of Americans being in Vietnam to help the Vietnamese was gradually forgotten, and more and more, the Americans were regarded as an army of occupation.

Unfortunately occupation was not the case with the military operations in the field. Americans did not occupy the ground over which they had traversed, either with or without contact. They went out to pursue and fight the enemy. But they did not go into any area with the idea in mind that they would stay there and hold the ground. The importance of maintaining a military presence was not considered. The operations were raids — and more often than not, when the operations came into an area, the Viet Cong could not be found. It was no wonder that the Americans began to think that the Vietnamese were revealing the timetable for the operations, and again the ugly feelings between the two allies were exacerbated. The Viet Cong seemed to take pleasure in not appearing when the Americans wanted them to stand and fight, but still it was a basic tenet of any army, guerrilla or otherwise, that you do not fight when the odds are against your winning.

From certain points of view, it appeared as though the tide had turned against the Viet Cong. The countryside that they formerly had run as they wished now was filled with large numbers of Americans on temporary marches, trying to find the track of the Viet Cong. Often the Americans did sweep into areas where they found honeycombs of the enemy's bivouacs; where, one by one, vast underground tunnel systems were destroyed, and where also food and medical supplies belonging to the enemy were ferreted out and put to the torch. But with very few exceptions, the war in Vietnam was an unreal war — in one month more men were killed and wounded by booby traps than were made casualties in pitched battles that resulted in a clear decision for one side or the other. And the longer the American operations continued, the more advance preparations they required, and hence the more chance that the enemy had of advance warning. The Vietnam war was different from any other war that the United States had fought, it was made up of a series of operations that had little connection with one another, that seemed to prove nothing new in the course of the war. There was, however, one notable exception — the array of operations did throw off the Viet Cong timetable. The enemy was set back to his old tricks of hitting the cities with terror — even inventing new ways of making the Americans uncomfortable such as the attack on Tan Son Nhut Air Force Base — and the fact remained that whenever the Viet Cong wanted to do damage, there was nothing that could specifically stop them. They had the support of the people in a way the United States did not. It took only fifteen to thirty men to succeed in getting to the world's busiest airport and to lob in mortar shells that knocked out a half-dozen aircraft permanently, damaged scores, and killed and wounded close to 100 American GI's.

What the Viet Cong had going for them was the fact that when they wanted to hurt, they almost invariably succeeded. The chronological development of the Viet Cong plan for victory had certainly suffered. And that was for the Americans the most reassuring aspect of our presence in Vietnam. The possibility of the Viet Cong's winning all of South Vietnam this year, or next, by military means no longer seems possible. The timetable for a Communist victory has been changed. And the theory that the Viet Cong were invulnerable in their jungle hideouts has also been proven wrong. The American operations have destroyed the myth that the jungle belongs to the Viet Cong. On the contrary, many of the American operations have been fought on Viet Cong's terms, in the Viet Cong's areas, and the Americans have come out winning the day. This is particularly true of the 173rd Airborne Brigade and the 101st Airborne who have gone into the Viet Cong's supposedly most invulnerable areas and pushed both the Viet Cong and the North Vietnamese out. The American Airborne proved the incorrectness of the theory that the Viet Cong could not be defeated on ground of their choosing. But the lost Viet Cong camps did not matter, nor did the destroyed enemy food and medical supplies — what did matter was breaking the enemy's morale, his belief that he could win.

Hundreds of thousands of Americans have been sent to Vietnam, but there is no evidence that the Viet Cong felt they were losing. Their timetable has altered, and the evolution of themselves from guerrillas into a conventional force that could take on anyone in a set-piece battle has also undergone a defeat. The Viet Cong have taken several steps backwards. They are again in the role of guerrilla and fighting as such — but in no way has South Vietnam gotten rid of its Viet Cong presence — if anything the Viet Cong are flourishing more determinedly than ever. Their radio voice is not silenced, nor is their claim that they will win. *That* is their objective, to win, to make South Vietnam their country, run their way — and that unquestionably means a Communist country — possibly reunited with North Vietnam, but even that is by no means certain. The only clear alliance between the Viet Cong and the North Vietnamese is that they want to rid their country of American influence. And they also will kill anyone who wishes the American presence to remain. If there were an American withdrawal tomorrow, one million South Vietnamese would certainly die in a purge, a million South Vietnamese who have thrown in their lot with the Americans. It should also be noted that the million South Vietnamese are a minority in a country of sixteen million people.

✻

America has described the war in Vietnam as limited, and defined the objectives as limited, too, although a candid explanation of our objectives is hard to find except that we refuse to abandon our "allies" to Communism. Since the time of the massive American buildup in Vietnam, the Vietnamese anti-Communist spokesman, the man who is our chief ally is Nguyen Cao Ky. His strength has grown with a dimension comparable to the vast United States commitment which by the end of 1966 had more Americans in Vietnam than were in Korea at the height of the fighting, had dropped more bombs than were dropped during the entire course of the Pacific War in World War II, had spent more than thirty billion dollars, lost more than 6,000 Americans, and had another 35,000 wounded. When Premier Ky speaks, he speaks as our ally, and when he acts, he has the support of the United States. He is Mr. Big in Vietnam. The issue is between Premier Ky and Ho Chi Minh, and Premier Ky is our man. When he arrived in Manila for the conference that for all intents was a war council for a long war, Premier Ky saw that all the heads of state had their own personal 707 jet. Premier Ky had only a Caravelle. He felt deprived, and he then systematically set out to get a 707 from the United States, and thought nothing of sabotaging the Pan American Airways in Saigon as a means of getting his own 707. Seldom in his life has Premier Ky not gotten what he wanted. He wants South Vietnam to become an anti-Communist country, and he wants the same for North Vietnam, too. Unlike most generals who have become victims of the vicious intramural fighting, Ky has shown extraordinary ability for survival and for improvement.

The variety of military dictatorships that had ruled in Saigon before Air Marshal Ky were all variations on one theme; there is one body of dependable strength in South Vietnam, and that is the military. As new leaders introduced themselves into the seat of power following the fall of President Diem, it was not a question of change in the structure of a military dictatorship. As one general expired and another took his place, it simply meant a changing of the figurehead. The guard was still the same. No one was particularly sad as one general stepped down to make room for another. No one got killed in the process, certainly not the generals who, once removed outside the country, could count on a generous living allowance; in many cases the official retirement pay of the deposed general was multiplied a number of times over by investments and such which were part and parcel of a general's due in Vietnam. It has not yet been proven that the Vietnamese generals die of starvation. Only the generals' ability at making investments differed from man to man, depending upon his own connections and to what degree he believed in channeling monies and securities outside the country into the safe and sanitary banks of Switzerland. Retiring a general happily is a Vietnamese institution.

And so, when I got to Vietnam, I took a keen interest in knowing what the Americans thought of Premier Ky. I was amazed at how little political importance they attached to him. They admired his reflexes as a fighter pilot. I would have liked to have heard someone volunteer something about Ky's political acumen. The expression most constantly used about Premier Ky was, "He's doing better than anyone thought he would do." Invariably I wanted to know better than what — and the immediate rejoinder to that was Premier Ky appeared to be enjoying himself a bit more than he had the month before in the role of Prime Minister. So it came out that in the beginning Prime Minister Ky was being obedient to the other generals in serving as Prime Minister. No one else wanted the job, either because they wanted a less prominent position where the light of scrutiny did not shine upon them, or they imagined the Prime Minister's seat as too temporary — generals were after all in the habit of using it recklessly in Vietnam. Prime Minister Ky was the compromise choice.

He was young, thirty-five years old, and he was unquestionably brave. He had led a fighter raid against North Vietnam, where he was born, and he had returned, bleeding in his cockpit seat, and was lifted out and borne off the airfield on the shoulders of his fellow pilots. He wore brilliantly colored scarves and preferred a rakish black Batman-like flying suit. The few words of caution uttered by the Americans in Saigon who were supposed to know were that Premier Ky was doing better than anyone had imagined by keeping a military government intact. There were some Americans who said he was too nice a guy for the in-fighting of the Prime Minister's job. Those who knew and liked him best were afraid that any day unexpectedly he would step down from the Prime Minister's job to go back to flying airplanes and bombing North Vietnam. When I asked why this would be such a terrible blow, they replied, to a man, "After Ky, there is no one else." They could not define Ky in any glowing terms, and they were fully cognizant of his daredevil character that would take on the most dangerous mission of aerial combat, but was not graced with the patience and the subtlety of a profound political leadership. In any case, the American attitude toward Premier Ky was that there could be no doubt about his loyalty to the idea of defeating the Viet Cong. He recognized the danger of a Communist takeover in South Vietnam, and there was nothing more important in American eyes than destroying that danger. Because he is so determined in pursuing the war, Premier Ky enjoys the confidence and even the gratitude of the Americans.

In many ways, Premier Ky is a creation of the Americans. He thinks big. He believes in fighting. He is anxious to prove the Vietnamese equal to any soldier in Asia, or in the world. He regards himself as a winner. He enjoys nothing more than spending an evening with his Air Force cronies, drinking, gambling, telling stories of bravery in aerial combat. At first his ambition for himself was limited to being the best aviator in Vietnam. And as with a serious pilot, and Premier Ky is indeed this, he is something of an artist, who daily finds expression, reality, and meaningful activity in flying. But flying is not enough any more. Now Premier Ky sees himself as the evangelical messiah who will reunite North and South Vietnam into one anti-Communist country.

Americans in the Embassy who support Ky think it providential that the Vietnamese are beginning to tell stories about Premier Ky as a sexual hero in Vietnamese popular folklore. The success of a political personality in Vietnam can be measured by the importance attached to his sexual prowess. The phallic male enjoys high virtue. Ho Chi Minh, for instance, is a legendary Don Juan who has no rival. And a number of stories with Premier Ky as the central god-king were gaining wide hearing. It was understood in these stories that Premier Ky loved his beautiful wife, a former stewardess of Air Vietnam, but that from time to time he could not ignore the flattery of some enchantress. On one such occasion, he had found himself in Hue, a city where there is widespread appreciation of beauty and love. Unfortunately, Mrs. Ky got wind of the escapade and flew to Hue, but before her plane could land, Premier Ky had been forewarned, and he told the control tower not to let the aircraft land on punishment of death. So a furious Mrs. Ky flew above the city while down below her husband carried on with his dalliance. Eventually, Mrs. Ky had to return to Saigon. The rebuke to the wife, of course, gave Premier Ky the advantage of face. His part in the story was that of the superior god, and everything would have been spoiled had the story ended with Mrs. Ky on the ground, neutralizing her husband.

These stories were told as fairy tales with a touch of ribaldry to give them spice; no one cared whether they were true or not, least of all the Americans. The Vietnamese, who believe in strong male personalities and often are quite plainly defeated by their equally strong-willed women, had the supreme satisfaction of hearing the story with the male predominant. As this diffused popularity for Premier Ky among the masses, the Americans did all in their power to see that such stories gained the widest audience, and they invited or encouraged more to be told in a similar vein. For all of this, it was somewhat depressing to be at a dinner party in the presence of the best American Embassy brains, and hear their regard for the phenomenon of the myth which inspired their own belief in Premier Ky. Somehow, it made me think that we were trying to justify the absence of political talent in Vietnam with stories of extraordinary sexuality. We appeared to be operating in a realm of myth, and no interpreter was required to realize that the myth did not solve the problems all around us — the electricity that failed, the bread that was filled with worms, the black market that thrived on thirty million dollars' worth of pilferage a year from the waterfront, and the overwhelming fact that the Viet Cong did not spread fairy tales. They had stricken almost 80 percent of Vietnam's physical landscape with either love or fear. Neither one was a parody of the truth.

＊

In calling Premier Ky to Honolulu, President Johnson was perpetuating the myth. In retrospect, the meeting was a blunder. It showed very little appreciation on the part of the people advising the President of the nature of Vietnamese attitudes, and a deplorable lack of insight into the makeup of the ten ruling generals. If all the generals had been invited, the blunder could have been avoided. The other generals would not have been jealous, and it would have shown that the United States understood the true nature of the ruling military junta. If you are going to give a party, which is what the United States did at Honolulu, you should invite all the principals, or the party will be spoiled. By bringing all the generals, we would have fused them a bit closer together and not divided them as happened. At the mere playback of the Honolulu Conference in Vietnam, every general began to give everybody else suspicious looks. They were all stricken with jealousy. Personal influence is all in Vietnam, and the President of the United States quite plainly had thrown his influence and power around Premier Ky. The generals being what they are, men who lead a certain group of men with arms, exist because of their personal power and the number of guns they have backing them up. There are degrees of power, to be sure; a Premier Ky can count on 400 airplanes to follow his commands. General Thi in the First Corps was capable of rousing thousands of men with guns behind him. The language these generals speak to each other is the language of the poker player. But when the generals saw one of the generals, the youngest, who had been placed in his position by their combined stakes of power, there was certain to be a reaction. In Premier Ky's case, there was also the fact that both *Time* and *Newsweek* magazines had placed him on their covers prior to the Honolulu Conference — and the reputation of both magazines in Vietnam is that they understand and shape the minds of the American people better than the people in Washington. In the dynamics of present-day Vietnam, the covers of *Time* and *Newsweek* are immortal. It's as if the scepter had been given to Premier Ky, and any doubt of it vanished when the Air Marshal flew to Hawaii for a summit meeting.

But as subsequent events in the wake of Honolulu showed, Ky destroyed Thi and every other general who chose to challenge him. By the spring of 1966, Ky, the reluctant Prime Minister, after tasting of the glories of Hawaii, showed no inclination to retire. He not only enjoyed the throne, he would not give it up. Ky proved himself powerful enough to carry himself and his supporters through one political and intra-military crisis after another. Far from being intimidated by the military uprising, and the tempestuous political actions of the Buddhists who saw the military rebellion within a civil war as their chance to seize power, Ky showed himself built of determination and courage in the face of any combination that sought to overthrow him. Piece by piece, he destroyed them. Everyone remembers the Buddhists sacrificing themselves by suicide with fire; the same shock tactics that had overthrown Diem did not work against Ky. For almost three months, the military government of Nguyen Cao Ky forgot about the war with the Viet Cong as it warred against street riots and insurrection. Ky survived, and his opponents were all defeated. It was said at the time that if the South Vietnamese want to keep a secret, they can. As if to prove it, Ky sent his troops north to Da Nang to put down the insurrection. The movement was accomplished without even the C.I.A. knowing about it. Ky, who is a North Vietnamese, ran into similar troubles just before the Manila Conference, when the civilian South Vietnamese cabinet members protested that his was a government of North Vietnamese, and that the South Vietnamese voice was not heard. Ky *is* NorthVietnamese, tough, aggressive, flamboyant, jealous, and a man who now believes that his talents will hold South Vietnam together, no matter what happens. He doesn't care about majorities or minorities, hence he believes that only a strong central authority can bring to Vietnam the unity it requires. Whatever emerges out of the so-called civilian government that is supposedly destined to replace the military junta, one thing is clear. Air Marshal Ky intends to supervise the running of that government, and if it goes against Ky's concept of *his* Vietnam, Ky will take whatever steps he deems necessary to displace it with something that he approves. For more than anything else, Ky feels he has a life tenure on being Vietnam's anti-Communist defender and protector.

This is one issue which all the talk of civilian governments seems to avoid, that Ky, a leader the Americans have created, is now like a Frankenstein, who has a mind and a desire of his own. He will, if necessary, turn upon his creator to fulfill his vision. Ky has ruled supreme in South Vietnam. He does so with one voice, the voice of guns, the only voice that so far has made decisions stick in Vietnam. South Vietnam possesses no serious opposition to Ky's strength except one, the Viet Cong, comprised of the Communists whom Ky has sworn to fight until he is dead. Both of them have one function. Both want one Vietnam, but ruled by different political concepts. Both have the gun voice. Their mutual desire to win is authentic. One will win, and one will lose. Coalition appears unlikely. Their strength is not identical. Even without the North Vietnamese, the Viet Cong could establish themselves militarily, then politically against Ky. But such is not the case today. The American military has produced an inequality of forces, and the chief beneficiary of the American commitment is not the peasant, not the economy, not the educational system of the Vietnamese, but the military forces that stand behind Premier Ky and his vision that a non-Communist country can be maintained in South Vietnam. If anything happened to Ky, if he were killed, who would take his place? Almost certainly another anti-Communist general.

✿

There was an apostolic gleam on the features of Vice-President Hubert Humphrey, his hand resting upon his chest as if in a moment of consecration, his other free arm about Prime Minister Ky of South Vietnam. They were standing together in the garden of the Saigon residence of Ambassador Henry Cabot Lodge. The Saigon press corps was well represented, and also present were the distinguished entourage of Washington correspondents following the Vice-President around. Vice-President Humphrey's words banished any sense of uncertainty from the hot tropical humidity.

There was an atmosphere of optimism in the fact that the United States was in Vietnam. These were times of promise, and the suggestion was full of medieval nuances, as if we had taken it upon ourselves to rescue the Holy Land from the infidel. This was a land in need of American goodness and charity. The American presence was a new era for these good people. No war had ever been holier, no enemy so colossally foul.

"We are not afraid," he said, flinging his arms open to the gathered press. The comparison to a political speech came to mind. The conduct of the Vice-President was that of a man on a campaign, speaking the kind of language which enables people to make up their minds about how to vote. There was a maximum of confidence, and the program of the entire morning was calculated to give the visiting newspapermen a feeling that the war in Vietnam was all but over. Somehow, it was all out of proportion to what was accurate, and none of the visiting Washington newspapermen I knew, Tom Wicker of the New York *Times*, Chuck Bailey of the Minneapolis *Tribune*, were taken in. It would have been more proper and more honest that morning if there had been less of the arrogance and the cockiness that is meant to melt the voter's heart and win his confidence and his vote. I felt considerable remorse because they had lined up a group of United States military advisers who did not seem too happy about the questionable honor of making their presentations to the assembled press. Each piece was the same. Things couldn't be better. There was no admission of weakness or errors, and one felt that the masking of what was actually happening in Vietnam was a deliberate pretense for the sake of the Vice-President. It appalled me to hear them conceal the most serious faults of our policy in Vietnam. The life of the advisers, as it was presented, appeared to be a bed of roses, with no sense of frustration or despair in their day to day relations with their Vietnamese counterparts. They kept talking about gains on every front, and there came back to me the fact that we were spending 600 million dollars a year in Vietnam for civilian efforts and rehabilitation, the biggest non-military aid anywhere in the world from the United States, and yet there was precious little to show for it. And the most unpardonable insult of all was that there was no mention of the ludicrous elements in the war, that we were flying B–52's against an enemy in South Vietnam that had no aircraft at all, and in the North we had lost over two hundred planes in twelve months, and that figure was still rising. The version of the war that was recited that morning in Saigon by the well-rehearsed American advisers for the sake of the visiting Washington correspondents was not the war I knew. Not that their accounts weren't accurate. They just were not the whole story. There was generous amplification of everything we hoped to do, but very little specific spelling out of what had been accomplished or lost in the course of American participation in the war. And that seems to be the danger that America is running in Vietnam. Our conclusions are one-sided. We are sharply limited in what we care to see. We ignore the difficulties en route to any given end, and only anticipate the end, without believing that we shall encounter difficulties getting there. Our hopes are not sufficient, nor our good intentions. We set to work believing, and at any point, when we are torn down, as happens more often than our being built up, we ignore what's happened. We don't recognize change. We keep projections of what we would like to see happen, but realities seem out of focus. We don't understand what the war means until we see one of our own dead returned to his family.

The total we looked at was ignorant of the destruction that was being done to the American soul and body and mind in Vietnam. What was difficult and dangerous to take was the fact that America's moral position in Vietnam was open to question. The fact is that ever since America came to Vietnam all we can faithfully claim for ourselves is an unbroken stream of heartbreak and contradiction. Nearly every non-military project that has been undertaken in the name of America makes a few people very rich and thousands of Vietnamese turn against us. The American presence in Vietnam has not cultivated any widespread appreciation for democracy. There are more Buddhists today who are advocates of neutralism than there are who would strike one blow for democracy. In a popular referendum, democracy would run a poor second to Ho Chi Minh. In the absence of anyone else, Air Marshal Ky became the symbol of what Vietnam lacks, the symbol of democracy.

✻

The task in Vietnam has been compared by some Washington spokesmen to the revolution that created these United States of America. But there are many differences between the Founding Fathers and the men who lead in South Vietnam today. The Founding Fathers were ignited by themselves. They knew what they wanted and they defined those wants in the Constitution, the Bill of Rights, and in the acts of sacrifice and devotion and inspiration that created the United States. Men who called themselves Americans brought to their dream their own belief. They counted on themselves, their brains, their wealth, and their courage. They did receive substantial help from France. If anything, there is more suitable comparison between the people of North Vietnam, fighting the present United States, and the colonial Americans who challenged the world's supreme power of their day, Great Britain. In other words, we are telling the people of South Vietnam, the ones who will listen, and they are not an overwhelming majority, what they should be and how they should go about being it. The men who wrote the Bill of Rights and the Constitution had no one peering over their shoulders telling them what to say and how to say it. They were speaking for themselves. They were prepared to fight a war. They believed in everything a war effort implied, and they had little hope of help from anyone outside. They planned to build a nation of their own definition. They were severing their ties with England, and they were creating their own notion of how to put together a country and run it. The people of South Vietnam are not choosing *this* war as *their* war. Today, they have no idea what kind of country it is they want. The creation, as it stands on paper, emphasizes the kind of country the United States would like to see there, but it is not necessarily the kind of country the Vietnamese want. In fact, beneath the surface, there is extraordinary bitterness among the people of South Vietnam at every escalation of American presence in their country. The present war is a war that has been imposed upon the people of South Vietnam, not through their own choice, but through the wishes of a few Vietnamese and the men who make policy in Washington.

Let us talk about what great wrongs have been done to the people of South Vietnam by the Viet Cong, who are South Vietnamese. South Vietnamese officials have been murdered by the Viet Cong. That is true. Much more than that, the Viet Cong have intimidated scores of villages into supporting them with food, money, and recruits. And it is also true that many villages in South Vietnam have welcomed and protected the Viet Cong, not as enemies but as liberators. The war in South Vietnam is a civil war. It has no reality if one describes it as a war of aggression.

More important is what the people of South Vietnam think about the war. They do not describe it as war against Communism. They see it as a civil war, as a power struggle between two rival factions of South Vietnamese, both seeking the seat of power, one representing a Communistic ideology, the other committed to a right-wing form of dictatorship which has the support of the United States.

The people of South Vietnam, furthermore, think of themselves as Vietnamese, as people who will one day be reunited with North Vietnam into one country. They feel that all the suffering of the present is for that final ultimate day when the one country will be a reality, and they do not consider what kind of government shall prevail. Insofar as systems of government are concerned, they do not care. They want to possess land without interference from foreigners. One thing is certain. Whenever the fighting is done, the United States will be presented with an enormous bill for damages from South and North Vietnamese, and the United States will be expected to pay that bill, large as it will certainly be. No ideologies will exist. The Vietnamese will be unanimous in demanding full and immediate payment from the party they hold responsible for the war, and that party is the United States.

How did our country get into the war to begin with? It was something that happened slowly. It was not a deliberate dramatic response such as President Roosevelt's when the Japanese *attacked* Pearl Harbor, nor President Truman's action when the North Koreans *crossed* into South Korea. It began in August, 1964, when U.S. Navy destroyers off the coast of North Vietnam were attacked by North Vietnamese torpedo boats. By February, 1965, President Johnson, as Commander in Chief, gave the order that started the bombing of North Vietnam. Today, it is clear that Vietnam is our war.

President John F. Kennedy advised us that it should be kept a Vietnamese war. He said, "In the final analysis, it is their war. They are the ones who have to win it or lose it. We can help them, we can give them equipment, we can send our men out there as advisers, but they have to win it, the people of Vietnam."

Let us face reality. It is now an American war. It has become our job to win it, not the job of the government of Premier Ky, whose army in 1966 had desertions totaling 110,000 men. American GI's are not in Vietnam as advisers. They are there, fighting a war that they feel is for *their* country, *their* flag, *their* Constitution.

We have inherited from the ill-fated French the role of defender of European non-Communist interests in the Far East, specifically in South Vietnam where we were supporting President Diem in establishing what amounted to a clearly anti-Communist regime, and a regime that at the same time was harshly fascistic in its domination of the people and free thought.

Without Diem, there would have been no Viet Cong. The Viet Cong were South Vietnamese who rose in protest against Diem. They had no other resources. Their government, such as it was, repressed any free expression under law, so the Vietnamese who became Viet Cong took the only way left to them. They declared themselves independent of Diem, and the Diem regime called them Communist outlaws. That the Viet Cong had Communist leadership and leanings is not to be denied: but the deeper cause of the Viet Cong's gaining such widespread popular appeal in South Vietnam was a direct reaction to the Diem regime, sponsored, protected, and financed by the United States. The struggle of the Viet Cong to free themselves and their country of Diem's influence was, by any standard, a laudable aspiration. If, indeed, the rise of the Viet Cong meant a Communist takeover of South Vietnam, it would only confirm what many believed would happen anyway — that South Vietnam and North Vietnam wanted to be Communist, that their choice in their new liberty from French domination was to align themselves with the Communist world. Such a decision was viewed with alarm in Washington, where decisions were made — certainly by the Chiefs of Staff and the

C.I.C. — on the basis that any action is defensible if it prevents Communist expansion in Asia.

The location of Vietnam is strategic. The coast of South and North Vietnam is 1200 miles long, the distance between Boston and Miami. Whoever occupies Vietnam has more than a toehold for any kind of military operation in Asia. If there were to be war between the United States and Communist China, possession of air and land bases in Vietnam would be vital to any military operations. That is why the Pentagon wants us in Vietnam, not for economic or commercial or social plans that will revitalize the Vietnamese people; but because in any long-range calculations for war with the Communist Chinese, it would aid us enormously to have bases in Vietnam. Vietnam is simply a pawn in the larger checkerboard of power plays between Washington and Peking.

Left alone, Vietnam would almost certainly become a small if not successful nation of Southeast Asia. The industrial potential of the North and the agricultural impact of the South would blend into a harmonious whole that would complement each other and bring to the thirty million people of Vietnam the prosperity and the peace they seek. But in reality, Vietnam is a small Balkan state of Asia, with an important access to Communist China, a border.

And so the question before all the powers gathered in confrontation in Vietnam is one of presence in Vietnam. No one cares as much about protecting the people of Vietnam as they care about protecting their own interests. Moscow will not lay aside the immense help it gives the people of North Vietnam because to leave North Vietnam means losing Russian presence in Hanoi, and it hurts China for Russia to be there. Equally, the Chinese encourage the North Vietnamese in fighting off the American planes and in doing combat with the Americans south of the 17th parallel because everything that divides Americans strengthens the Chinese.

Vietnam provides an arena for power plays, and by that token it is like the Spanish Civil War all over again for the great atomic powers of the sixties, powers that are preparing for a war. Vietnam is the testing ground. It is a dropout from the family of nations, because in no way has Vietnam been given the chance to develop in whatever was its natural course — whether Communist or non-Communist, whether to be in the Soviet Camp, or Peking's satellite, or to develop, as many believe it would, had it been left alone, into a Tito-like country of Southeast Asia. With the fear of a Communist take-over in all of Southeast Asia and the fear of a third major war with Communist China, the United States, under the false shelter of humanitarian reasons, began moving into

Vietnam to throw up a military barrier against losing what essentially are vital land bases for any war that might ensue in the forthcoming decade. Above all, the only feasible authority for the United States being in Vietnam is this, the military consideration that American presence in Vietnam might conceivably reduce the odds of that future war.

American presence in Vietnam means that Peking is bound to be hurt in any future war. This is what I think the Vietnam war is all about. It is not a war for justice for the Vietnamese. Its purpose is not to make a brave new world for the people of Vietnam. The war in Vietnam is unhappily a preliminary to a larger war, and in such a preliminary, the guilt and responsibility for the deaths of the innocent falls upon the United States. The Vietnamese believe this, Communist or non-Communist, and they bitterly resent our being there. Because the Chinese are not seen in the South, they are not held to blame. I do not believe that many people in South Vietnam are grateful for our being there as a military power. The people, if they could actually express their feeling, would ask us to leave, because then they would feel that the end of the war would appear immediate.

We are not trying to seize territory from the Vietnamese people. We are, in the new context and idiom of this atomic age, paying a heavy price to guarantee that the territory of Vietnam is not denied us if we need it for war against China. The story of Vietnam is one of turmoil and strife to rid itself of foreign European presence so they could determine whatever their future could be. Their personal task of finding themselves has been made impossible by the present war. The Vietnamese are not leading their own lives; if they were, they would have held an election on whether to unite or separate. They would have fought their wars among themselves; and it is certain that many tens of thousands of them would have died deciding the issue, but the decision to fight would have been their own, and not ours.

The tremendous military power of the United States is not focused in Vietnam against a major adversary. The Chinese Communists, for instance, are training an entire generation of their young people to hate the Americans. They are preparing their people toward an eventual confrontation with this country. There is a definite promise that Peking intends to wage a war against the United States. There is hate, uncertainty, mistrust, envy, and revenge in every contact between America and the Chinese Communists.

Yet, the grand act of war is now focused upon the people of North Vietnam and the rebels of South Vietnam. It is not a war to make justice, but a war that creates further injustice, and it leaves behind it a wrecked country and a people that now begin to look upon America with the same savage mistrust that has collected deep in the heart of Communist China.

And the sadness of it all is that the true enemy, Communist China, sits back and watches Americans die at the hands of a weak inexperienced new nation called North Vietnam and its allies, the rebel forces of South Vietnam.

6. PRIVATE WAR

At mail call Dodson had a letter that day and he saved it as usual for the evening. He liked it better then because he felt that was when he really talked to her, when he saw her, and heard *her* voice. He was also curious about his boy, a boy he had never seen; still, he was taken up with the pride of fatherhood in absentia. He had been in Vietnam for ten months, and he was getting short in the time he had left. Two more months, sixty days, and he would go back home and see *her* and *their* son. He walked into the tent he shared with his buddy, and he looked up at the wall where there was a realistic-looking cartoon of a nude woman. Tiny numbers were speckled all over her anatomy. The cartoon belonged to his buddy. The legs were filled in with colored crayons, as were the arms and the breasts. All of her, except for the part around the navel and down into the crotch. In another month she would be covered and his buddy would be going home.

Dodson didn't have a short-timer's girl calendar. He didn't need it. He knew to the minute how much time he had left.

His billet wasn't too bad. He had a cot and a mosquito net, comfortable enough for a Marine.

He and his buddy seldom got into any discussion about the war in profound detail as to why they were there. His buddy was white, and Dodson was a Negro, but there was no distinction in that. They were both sergeants, and what they talked about was the Marine Corps or their men or which officers they liked and which they didn't. They weren't discreet about the problem of race because there was no problem here. Dodson was ambitious and he had made sergeant. The rank meant a great deal to him. He didn't feel quite the outsider that some of the other Negroes of his experience had described. May be that's because he was born in York, Pennsylvania. And he was a reasonably happy man, who courted no sympathy because of his skin, but wanted respect for what he was.

His hours that were his own were spent reading his wife's letters. And even though he knew them all by heart, he still reread them because he never felt alone talking to her through the letters. In some ways that he couldn't ever tell anyone, he felt his identity was locked up with the letters. Publicly, he was to Vietnamese and Americans what the stripes on his arm said: a Marine sergeant. But when he opened the little metal box and took out the letters, he was unsealing that part of himself that was most private, and which he loved more than anything else, the little baby of the pictures and the words his wife sent him. They were his family. He put the new letter in the box, unopened, but he looked at the postmark, and he saw that it said 10 A.M., May 1. He thought of her, going shopping and dropping it in at the post office. He locked the letter in with the others, thinking how much he loved her and the son whom he had never seen.

The sun was bright outside the tent. It was that way most of the time in Da Nang, except in the winter months, when the rains came, and sludged everyone into an apathetic dampness.

Dodson put on his Marine fatigue hat with its peak and its stiff visor. The hat looks awkward on anyone but an authentic Marine. It is reminiscent of a Russian revolutionary cap, and the more experienced the Marine who wears it, the more it acquires a vintage dash, elegance, and authority. Dodson wore his like a professional. He carried his M–14 rifle with the finesse of a man who had fired it in combat. As a member of the 3rd Engineer Battalion, Third Marine Division, Dodson had seen combat around the Da Nang perimeter, and once, in a fire fight, he had been hit in the leg by Viet Cong bullets. He had lain on a hospital cot and received the Purple Heart for the wound.

He had come to Vietnam prepared in his mind to endure whatever fighting there was to be done. But he had seen men die in action, and he was glad that he was able to walk. He was not tall and not short. His body was tight and compact and his skin was very black. He was a good-looking man with straight features that expressed conviction beyond his twenty-three years of age. He had in his walk the quality of a man who is not subject to tyranny, whatever its form. He was no by-product of a man. He wished only to do his job, and to do it well. So he strode now toward the road construction gang of which he was boss.

The road had no name. It was part of the extending Marine perimeter south of Da Nang. As the Marines pushed out from the coast, they built roads to make it easier for truck convoys to reach the farthest outposts. The road was as conspicuous a sign as could be found of Americans pushing farther inland. It suggested to friend and foe that the Viet Cong were losing, not overnight, but slowly, that they were renouncing land they had lost in many conflicts — small scattered clashes, night ambushes, battles that had no name where men were killed and wounded, as already Dodson had been wounded. And to the building of the road, the Americans were lending precision and permanence, contemplating a time when traveling across the land would no longer be dangerous. The road changed the landscape. It was American. And it was a stage, progress toward the day when the Viet Cong would be afraid to show themselves, day or night. It was neat and wide, a formal path across the green paddy fields. The American road went like an arrow into the land where the Viet Cong, in more than one sense, belonged. The road was also supposed to be an outstretched arm, inviting the peasants to follow it back to where the Americans presided. But the road was barren in the heat. There was no one on it except the Marines, working to extend it farther. They were their own company, and they were the only perceptible witnesses of their progress. Their work was not enlivened by the presence of children watching or peasants thanking them for having come to build the road. The scene of the Marines working alone was reminiscent of a lonely prison gang breaking rock. Most of the Marines were white, and the boss was a Negro, Sergeant Dodson.

He moved down past the circle of men digging with pick and shovel and they passed greetings to one another. The Marines were progressing to his satisfaction, and because it was hot he didn't say much, and they didn't either. It was also part of his way not to say much, not to use his rank unless he saw something he didn't like. And then he would speak out and give it to them so that his words fell like a lash of contempt on their weakness. But now he was silent. He looked out ahead to where the road was going, passing just this side of a village where he could see women and children. He thought that Vietnamese villages were sorrowful in the way there were always many women and children, but few, if any, men. The men, who were the fathers, lovers, sons, or brothers, had vanished, and the few who remained were old, distinct in their age and infirmity.

He realized what the war was about, knowing that the road was a start toward the village. Dodson had done his homework. He knew that in this war the Marines were different, and he didn't question the difference, long for the sands of Iwo Jima, consider it less than right that Marines were compromised when they had to fight where there were people and villages. The fighting, he thought, justified the building that had to come afterwards, and even when they got together back at the camp and talked about it, the way Vietnamese people were hostile and didn't trust the Marines, the more they argued in favor of this other thing that had to be done, this encountering the people on their terms, and winning their trust.

Deep in himself, Dodson sometimes likened the situation in Vietnam to what was happening at home. On one side was the Negro, and on the other, the white man. And the far side was the promise. Dodson didn't believe that the way to the promise could be found easily. But he was sure that he would make it there. That's why he was in the Marines. He also believed that his pattern was not everyone's pattern, and people had to be helped. And that's what the Marines were doing in Vietnam, working their way through a forest of mistrusts.

Building the road, he believed, was a way of acquainting the Marines with the people and vice versa. The labor, the expense, the danger was worth it, if it would bring peace to the land.

He thought these things and he headed toward the village. He was alone.

The walk across the paddy field was a gentle walk, with water buffalo off in the distance, a couple of children riding on the backs of the buffalo, idle. The weather was fine, the fields were green and lush, and he felt that there was nothing better than being a Marine working to make a land peaceful.

He passed into the village and distinct before him were two women sitting on the ground, nursing young babies, quiet and gentle, enough to make him think of the unread letter waiting for him under his cot. Elusive were the sounds in the village, a rushed voice of hungry mouths fastened on cheek-like breasts, and the air passing through the trees, and the scent of secluded rustic smoke, and the hollow sound of foliage breaking somewhere near, an inquisitive sigh like a letter sealed and dropped in a mailbox. He made an effort to listen. The village was overshadowed by the trees, the wood-thatch houses were built close together, and sunlight fell like something pagan and secret down through the ceiling of mournful expansive black branches.

Curiosity drew him on, if not his own sense of what he was, a Marine sergeant; he wanted to know what was in the village. He moved into the deeper darkness, where there was no sun, behind the houses.

Then it was as if the noise spit at him. The day was smashed into light, and he knew that something, someone had hit him on the head. He fell to the ground, and as he did, he saw coming out of the forest darkness, the first man, a young man dressed in black pajamas. The Viet Cong. The enemy.

He staggered to his feet, suddenly realizing that they wanted him, and then it was too late. He fell again, dropping his rifle, and then he realized that he had not dropped it. It had been grasped out of his hands by someone else behind him. So there were two; he caught a brief glimpse of the man behind him. He knew he had to fight, and it mattered to him not to be captured. He made a grab for the rifle of the man who was now above him. But the blow had hurt him, or the enemy was too fast. The rifle escaped him, and then there was another blow on his head.

He made one more desperate attempt to grab at a Viet Cong's ankles, and the man swerved aside. They had him flat on the ground now, and he was focusing better. He could see six men, and they all looked alike with yellow faces and dark hair. They were small, but they were strong. Once more he tried to wrestle free, and this time one of them hit him hard across the face and Dodson groaned, not so much from the pain, but knowing they had him beat.

"Quiet," one of them whispered, in English. "We no kill. Quiet."

Dodson wondered whether they had planned the ambush this way, watching him cross the field and come into the village. Or had it just been rotten luck? He didn't know. They tied a rope around his hands, and as they were doing that, another was taking off his boots. The ambush was not an accident, he thought. They were not excited, or anxious. They seemed pleased.

They jerked on the rope, a long ten-foot rope, and Dodson knew what it meant; they wanted him to get up. They looked back at him, trying to fight from getting to his feet, and one of them raised his rifle, and pointed it at Dodson. Another one came close and poked a rifle into Dodson's ribs. He didn't need any more urging. He'd rather stay alive and figure it out later when his head was clear and he had a better chance. He would go with them. Wearily he stood up. His bare feet rested on the scratchy ground. He had a yen to yell, but he checked it with them so close and the Marines too far away to do him any good. He thought he was dreaming, but then they yanked on the rope, and they started running, pulling him like an animal, and they ran past the women, innocent as ever, feeding their babies. They pulled him into the jungle and he wondered if he would ever get back to Da Nang.

They had bound his hands well, and as they ran through the jungle he tried to work his wrists free, but there was no chance of sliding them out. He knew that they were taking a track away from the road, from Da Nang, and up into the mountains where the Viet Cong had many hideouts. Their running pace was steady and silent and he tried braking them down slower once and he got another crack across the head. They were hard cool customers, and after that he stayed with them, still feeling like something alien, running and sweating, and feeling the bonds around him this way. And he wondered if this was the way it had been in Africa, when the slave traders came and captured his ancestors and took them through the jungles to the coast. "*Run, run, run,*" he whispered to himself, knowing that each step took him farther away from his own people, three of them in front, three in back, the seven of them, running Indian file. Once in a while there was a murmur from one to the other but he didn't know what they were saying. Dodson wished now that he knew Vietnamese and had taken the language course the Marines had just started.

✲

About an hour later, they reached a river. The one pulling at his rope pointed to the boat that was there, indicating that Dodson was to get in. He was suspicious of the boat because that meant more distance away from Da Nang, and so he moved slowly, and his hesitation prompted another glancing blow. He sat in the boat, and then when they were all in, they moved slowly away from the shore and they went along the river for a while. He sat there silent and sullen until they reached a point on the opposite bank where they landed, and there were more Viet Cong, all in black pajamas, all armed.

The leader of the band who had met them came close to Dodson and he said, in a halting English, "Do you speak Vietnamese?"

Dodson moved his head in the negative.

"We will not harm you, if you obey us," said the leader.

Dodson stared into the man's eyes and couldn't see anything in the slits to make him believe or disbelieve the statement. Many more Viet Cong had come out of the bush and they jammed in close, feeling his muscles and fingering his fatigue jacket. He saw nothing in their faces but curiosity, and he assumed that for now they had no intention of killing him. Then the commander shrieked and they all backed away. They disappeared into the bush; they seemed unconcerned about there being any threat here. Dodson looked up into the sky. It was bright blue and there were no airplanes anywhere. The sound of the river was louder than anything else. He heard no planes, not even the distant buzz of a light observation aircraft, prowling around looking for Charley. Well, thought Dodson, I've sure found them. He looked down at his feet, scratched and bloody from the run. He tasted salt in his mouth, and he realized how thirsty he was, but he didn't want to ask them for a drink of water. They knew he was a Marine, and he wasn't showing them he was a tenderfoot. He wanted to lie down, but they were all standing, talking to the leader, so Dodson waited, moving his toes. He wondered where they would take him now. By now, the Marines back on the road would have missed him and they would have gone into the village, and found nothing there but those mothers and their babies. He could feel how empty the village would be of any sign of him. They would have wiped away the tracks and the signs of the scuffle, and the village would look defenseless. They wouldn't know how he had been dragged off. And it made his spirits sag to think of the letter he had not read.

Then the leader walked off and only four Viet Cong were left. They pulled on the rope and dragged Dodson after them, in another direction, along the banks of the river. Once he could hear the wail of children from somewhere near but he saw nothing. They picked up the pace, back to running, and he kept up with them at the desired speed. His legs felt strong and it didn't bother him that his feet were bare. There was no talk. Just the sound of their feet padding along with the pace and rhythm of racers in a marathon that has just begun and the runners are conserving their strength for the time when one is ready to push ahead of the pack. Dodson kept telling himself that he must remain alert for a way to escape; he told himself that if he did not, he would disappear as casually as a wave drowns a man.

They went on, away from the river, up into the jungle-covered hillside. They were on a trail that twisted without any meaningful pattern. There was no difference in the terrain, the trees were huge and high, carrying up into a tangled overgrowth. And there were more thorns here and his feet were bleeding again.

When night came there was no moon, but still the Viet Cong kept up the pace, running in the strange oppressive silence of the jungle, and it was like running down one darkened corridor into another one, empty of everything except thick black night.

✸

Sometime in the night, they lay down. They put Dodson in the middle, and they tied his rope to a tree. They gave him rice and water and then they sat up talking, their voices more often than not in whispers, but when they laughed, it was a screaming laughter like parrots cackling.

Dodson tried not to sleep, thinking that his chance might come. But when their voices fell silent, three rolled over. One remained on guard. Dodson listened to the whistling of the man on watch.

The guard was about thirty, and his eyes stared straight into Dodson's. His look was alert and suspicious, watching the way a cat watches. Even though it was dark, the Viet Cong's eyes were like glints of steel focused on the prisoner. Dodson turned away, and the night descended on him, the shape of the foliage swayed above him, and he stared up, listening to the murmur of wind in the trees. He saw himself running in slow motion, and then gratefully Dodson fell asleep.

❋

Dodson leaped up out of his sleep, and then he was tugged down by the rope and the heave the guard had given it. Dodson blinked at the guard and he saw that it was light and he wasn't going anywhere but where they wanted to take him. He couldn't remember his dream, but he had awakened expecting something other than this. One of the guards moved up to him with rice and water. As soon as Dodson had it before him the man backed away. They ate their breakfast, and Dodson ate his, managing as best as he could. He barely lifted the canteen cup to his lips, tilting it up carefully with his bound wrists so that he wouldn't waste it. He ate the rice, using his mouth more than his hands. They didn't notice. They ate with gulping slurping sounds and sighs of satisfaction. Dodson guessed he had slept for five hours. Then they were on the move again.

The sky was pale and shy and the Viet Cong were in a hurry. They set the same running clip they had maintained yesterday.

By mid-morning they reached a village, the first of a number they were to pass in the next three days. All of the villagers came out to see the prisoner, and what was marked about these villages to Dodson was the number of able-bodied young men. They were armed, uniformed, obviously living with their families and helping with the farming or whatever job was to be done. There were more than fifty armed young men, and Dodson knew now that they had entered the heart of Viet Cong territory. It worried him how he could escape.

I should have paid more attention to the direction we were taking, he blamed himself. It would be difficult by any measure to get away now. He must pay attention to details.

This was like any other village with the picture of Buddha on an altar-like stand where incense burned, and dogs scuffling everywhere, and chickens running wild. And yet there was order. A Viet Cong flag hung over one house; inside Dodson could see stacks of American C–ration cartons and what he recognized as cases of ammunition and hand grenades. The house was full of stuff, and then one Viet Cong crossed over and offered Dodson a cigarette from a fresh package of L & M's. Dodson thanked him with a smile and didn't take it. The Viet Cong shrugged and lighted the cigarette with a Zippo lighter, flicking it shut with a smart click just like someone who had been used to Zippos all his life.

Even though they were all staring at him, he didn't feel shame in his position. He didn't taste shame. In his mind, he would get out of this. He had to keep that in sight and then they couldn't shame him. It was important to Dodson that he hadn't accepted a one-way ticket to their land. His place was back there, in Da Nang, and it grew in him, stronger than before, that he would return.

The people around him seemed friendly. They offered him bananas. He took one. He could tell from their chatter that they were wondering how he would peel it, and he moved as cautiously as if he were defusing a dangerous mine, taking the peel off with his teeth, remembering that if he dropped the banana they would think less of him. Something told him this. He had never read it. And it gave him a sense of pride when he had peeled it.

The banana was in his fingers, his wrists were, of course, still tied by the rope, a rope that now lay on the ground with no one holding on to it, because they knew, and Dodson knew, that he wasn't going anywhere. To his horror, he felt his fingers shaking as he ate the banana but it was so slight that only he could tell. And he was glad that they couldn't tell. That would have shamed him.

"What do you think of this place?" said one of the black pajamas. Dodson expected them to speak English. He was conscious of voices interpreting the question and the scrutiny in all the faces around him, waiting for his answer.

"It's fine," he said, smiling and looking at the children.

He said what he felt.

"It's fine," he repeated. He hadn't heard them interpret what he had said. "It's fine," he said, again, slow, so they could understand.

The Vietnamese words were spoken.

It was like a splash of water on his face when they laughed and smiled and an old woman came up and gave him a C–ration cracker. He munched on it, smiling at them, and they smiling at him.

They marched for two more days and two more nights, always up higher, and the nights got colder, and whenever they came to a village, they displayed Dodson. There wasn't anything he objected to in being displayed because they never tried to hurt him. They never took the rope off his wrists, as if they felt that by having his hands bound they had insurance he was their captive. Every time they came to the villages submerged in the jungle, they would let go of the rope; and each time, Dodson was in the foreground. They fed him, they gave him water, and they did not hit him. He had no idea what they were considering doing to him when they got to wherever they were going, but he took care now as they went along, holding in his mind landmarks that would tell him direction for the day when he hoped to come back alone. The idea of escaping lurked deep within him, and he knew that when the time came, it would be a quick occasion, when cunning as well as courage would be needed. His feet were getting tougher. He only worried about getting them infected because then he wouldn't be able to move; so whenever they came to a stream, he soaked them in the cold water and held to the idea that anything clean wouldn't be troubled with infection.

And all the time the language of the jungle became a language he began to understand. The dark didn't launch any fear in him because he felt he could see in it if he let it embrace him, and he was not afraid. He understood the language of the jungle; how when the noises above, the monkeys or birds, quieted, someone was moving, and it was a special feature of the Viet Cong that they could run in the jungle, not making more than one constant sound that didn't frighten all the bird and animal noises into going silent too. Everything about that trek stayed in Dodson's memory because sometime, he promised himself, he would be alone, and they would be chasing him. He didn't know when it would be, but the day would come. Once in a while, thinking about it, he would lag and then they would pull on the rope viciously, and the pain stayed deep in him that he was their prisoner. He would get back into step with them, keeping their beat and their pace and all the time, secret in him, was that other life. It stayed within him.

✿

They came into the camp in the morning hours, ahead the two, then the prisoner, then the other two. They came into it running, because the guards counted on what they would look like to the camp. They wanted no stories told about them as tired or trembling. And Dodson caught on to what they meant, so he did not cramp their style or hang back. He ran, like a Marine, not a prisoner, because he didn't want any of them to think he couldn't take it. He didn't want them to think he was chastised.

He knew he had come to the end of the journey because they had told him, in a sign language, that this was the camp.

It was not a big camp, but it was high up in the mountains. There was one other rise back of it, rocky and jagged, and the wind blew down and flogged away the heat.

He was untied and brought into a hut where there were other prisoners, all South Vietnamese Army, uniformly tired-looking and not much interested in the new man. The camp obviously had been set up for keeping prisoners. There was no sign of the normal village life, no women, no animals, no crying babies.

Dodson looked around for other Americans and he saw none. The prisoners in the hut were all South Vietnamese and he counted them. Eleven. Eleven detached, disinterested faces. He distrusted them. He could not work with them. He came to this understanding with himself almost immediately. He was acting not out of any guiding principle, but simply that he had to play it alone. Alone, at least, he was intact.

In the closeness of the prisoner hut, he found a corner, and he made it his own. It was impossible to stretch out luxuriously, but it was his piece of ground.

He looked at his feet. There wasn't any part of the skin that hadn't been broken or bruised. The soles were grimy and calloused and marked with blood.

He rubbed them with his hands now free of their bonds. But the fact that he was a prisoner was still with him.

He had no blanket. No one did in the hut. But the Vietnamese stayed close together, all in a huddle of their own warmth. He lay there, and he felt cold. The wind was loud outside, but no matter, he heard the sound of a radio. He listened and made out music that wasn't American and he thought of the Supremes, the Motown sound, and for a brief spell, he heard it in his mind. Maybe they were listening to the American radio.

He sat up, hoping that he could hear better. He was disappointed when he waited, silent, listening, and the music came to him as the foreign-sounding dissonance of Vietnamese. They were not playing a record, of that he was sure, because there was static, and that meant a radio. They were enjoying it though. He heard them clapping their hands in time to the music. They were enjoying it.

He thought about his cot and the box with the letters. He set his mind to remembering what his wife had written. He didn't move. He thought, and it came back to him. The son he had never seen was locked in his mind and his heart, and now as if the son were there beside him, he could see him. He didn't dare move because if he did, it would all be lost, and he knew that his wife and his son were not a dream. They were the rope around him that would get him out. He belonged to them. He swore to himself that he would get away.

He would never be happy until he got out.

He lay on his back. He didn't feel empty. He would study it. He would get away. The wind blew into the prisoner's hut and Dodson, lying there, believed in what he was telling to himself. He would find a way to get back.

*

The prisoner's house was awakened in the morning when one of the Viet Cong guards came in, shouting in Vietnamese, and beating on a bamboo tube that made a bullet-like sound. Dodson dove when he heard it because he thought he was in a fire fight, and his reaction led to laughter. Dodson didn't like that. He was a sergeant in the United States Marine Corps, and he didn't want them to laugh at him and he felt bitter. They spent an hour in what Dodson gathered was supposed to be exercise, going out where the crooked slope was windswept. A small Viet Cong who had something wrong with his back, some kind of disfigurement that wasn't quite a hunchback but gave him a distorted set of shoulders, was in charge. Dodson thought of him as the chief.

Next, the prisoners were escorted back into their hut. The Vietnamese were given pamphlets and newspapers to read, but since everyone knew Dodson didn't know the language, he was ignored. The interior of the hut was light enough in the day so that everyone had no trouble reading.

One of the ARVN prisoners came over and sat next to Dodson.

"You a Marine?" he said, in rather good English.

"Yes," said Dodson. He looked at the man and saw someone who was about twenty-five.

"You are special prisoner," said the Vietnamese, speaking in a whisper.

"What do you mean?"

"They may bring you to the North."

"To the North?"

"Yes. To Hanoi."

"You mean I'd have to run all the way up there?"

"How do you mean run?"

"That's how we got here. Running."

"I think that they have a plan to exchange Americans. To use you."

"No."

"Yes."

"How do you know this?"

"They like to boast. They will," and looking over his shoulder to see that the guard was not observing them, and satisfied he was not, the South Vietnamese continued, "they will be promoted for having American prisoners."

"We have a plan," said the South Vietnamese.

"How do you mean?" said Dodson.

"The plan is to cooperate."

"Why?"

"Because they will give us better food and treatment, blankets against the cold, medicines when we are sick. Are you with us?"

"Cold up here," said Dodson. The prisoner hut had taken on an air of danger. The man could be a plant put there by the Viet Cong to feel him out. Dodson played it cool. He didn't want to shut the door on an opportunity to escape; but if the man intended to use him, all Dodson could think was, shit on that.

"How old are you?" asked the Vietnamese.

"Twenty-three," said Dodson.

"Are all Americans young?"

"We don't worry," said Dodson.

He decided that he wouldn't trust anyone yet; he could hardly tell the difference between this man and the Viet Cong. They looked alike. So he sat there, silent, and he was relieved when the Vietnamese left him and rejoined the others in the hut. Dodson had read enough about secret police to be suspicious. He was aware also that he was in enemy country, a prisoner, and that these people spoke the same language, and that put him at a disadvantage.

Dodson thought he hadn't been very friendly. But he also felt he had to be careful. In this country, he knew, the friendliest faces could be the enemy, and he remembered the women feeding their babies when he had been captured.

A few days passed and nothing important happened to Dodson. He was not approached again by the Vietnamese. He lived in his own corner of the prisoner hut, hoping that they were not thinking of bringing him North. If they did, he would have to make a break somewhere on that march, somewhere when he figured they were near Da Nang because once across the border into the North, he would never have a chance. He recalled a talk from a Marine who said there was a way of holding your wrists slightly wide apart when they were tied, so that you had room to work loose. He was going over it in his mind when the Viet Cong guard came and got him.

"He says for you to go with him," said the English-speaking Vietnamese.

Dodson followed the guard out of the hut.

Dodson froze. In the group of Viet Cong just ahead was a young white face. He was a Marine, dressed as Dodson was in green fatigues, and his feet were bare. His face was young and there was a fuzz of beard on his chin. He had delicate features and a longer shock of hair than most Marines. He was not a big man. He looked like a kid, and Dodson expected that he was seeing things, and that if he blinked and looked the Marine would not be there. Dodson shifted his eyes up to the high ground where there was sunlight, like a tinge of happiness above the prison camp.

Then he heard the voice: "Hi."

"Nice to see you," said Dodson.

"Same here," said the Marine.

They shook hands.

"How long you been here?"

"Two days," said Dodson.

He still couldn't get used to the idea that this was indeed an American, a Marine like himself.

"Where they catch you?"

"Right near Da Nang."

"Me, too."

They both smiled, smiled at the incongruity.

The Vietnamese spoke up, "You two are to go with this guard. They want the doctor to look at your feet. They say you are to do nothing foolish. They will not kill you."

They were taken to a building that was a dispensary, where there was a Viet Cong doctor wearing a white uniform. He had a young male assistant who wore the ordinary black pajamas. The room was clean and remarkably well equipped with shelves of medicines and bandages, surgical instruments, an operating table, and looked, in fact, not much different from what a Marine would expect at a forward aid station. A good many of the supplies bore American labels. There were also surgical instruments and Dodson knew they were sharp.

The doctor said quietly, "Sit down. I will look at your feet."

They sat down on a bamboo bench, and the doctor examined the cuts, blisters, and bruises on their feet, and then gave directions to the assistant.

The assistant filled two battered pans with a solution from a couple of bottles, and he put them before the two Marines.

"Soak," said the doctor.

They put their feet in the pans, and then the doctor said, "Nothing serious."

He looked at his watch, and he said something again to his assistant.

"He will give you a bottle of some antiseptic, and some cotton, and you apply it. In a few days, you will have no problems." Then the doctor looked at the two Marines, "I am a professional." Then he gave some more instructions to his assistant and taking off his white gown, he walked out. He was wearing a pistol belt with a forty-five at his hip. The assistant went out, and Dodson quickly stole a small knife off the table.

The two Marines were escorted back to the hut where Dodson had slept, and Dodson was grateful that the new man was going to share the same hut with him. He had been worried ever since he had met the young Marine that they would be separated. If they tried to do that, he would have tried anything, pleading, raging for them to stick together.

Inside the hut, Dodson showed the man where he was staked out, and there was more than enough room. And then they sat there, and for the first time, Dodson heard how the new man had been captured.

His name was Lance Corporal Walter W. Eckes. He was twenty years old, and he came from New York City. Eckes was a radio operator with an artillery forward observer team, attached to C Company, Ninth Marine Regiment, Third Marine Division.

The two Marines bent their heads together, and Eckes began to tell his story.

"I can't tell you what a surprise it was," said Eckes, "them taking me right in sight of Da Nang. I mean you wouldn't expect it there."

Dodson shook his head in understanding. He knew the feeling well.

"Tell me about it," said Dodson.

"I was hitchhiking back to my company CP. I was up at regimental headquarters, and you know, just routine, I was hitchin' a ride, just like we always do."

Dodson could recall easily the sight of the Marines on the roads, near Da Nang, slouching along, identified with the area, carrying their weapons, and probably a lot of things on their minds, but not the idea of becoming a prisoner. You wouldn't think that the Viet Cong would dare it so close to where there were fifty thousand Marines.

Eckes rubbed his chin, scratching at the beard growing there.

"It was morning, hot and sticky, and the road was dusty as hell, but I couldn't see any trucks coming, but down the road were these three ARVN. They were dressed like the ARVN are, kind of sloppy, and they were holding their weapons over their shoulders, the way they do, you know, holding onto the barrel, with the stock up back. It never occurred to me they were anything but three old ARVN coming back from a night out cattin' round. Good luck to them, I thought. Then, they come right up to me, I mean close, and I'm still looking for a ride, and the one of them swings his rifle off his shoulders, and he points it right at my belly. And the other two jumped me. Before I could do anything, they'd taken my forty-five I was carrying, so there I was without my gun. They tied me up, I mean my hands, and they just pulled me off. At first, I wasn't sure but that they were drunk. I wasn't sure they were VC, but about a half-hour later they took me to this village, and I saw the Viet Cong flag, and I knew they had me. That's when they made me take off my boots. And we just been running all the way here. They're crazy, the way they make you run through the damn jungle. Christ, the D.I.'s ought to have a session with these guys."

Dodson said, "Ain't that the truth."

He was relaxing. It was comfortable to be with a Marine. To talk the same language. To know who the man was. To trust him.

"Listen," said Eckes, "you're a sergeant, and I'm a Marine, and I guess I call you sarge, right?"

"You call me Jim, okay, Wally?"

"Okay, Jim."

And Dodson was thinking, when we get back to the Corps, it will be the Corps. Right now, we're just plain Marines, and we got a lot of business ahead of us.

❄

They never talked about escape in the daytime when they were afraid that the ARVN would overhear and spoil it. But at night, when they lay down together, side by side in the hut, and were as close to one another as a man and woman keeping each other warm, they would whisper into each other's ears. And if the ARVN thought they were lovemaking, all the better.

"Wally," said Dodson.

"Yeah."

"I want to get out."

"You got a plan?"

"Not yet. But I got a knife for when the time comes."

"You think we can?"

"Yes."

"How?"

"I don't know. We got to wait."

"Okay."

"You with me?"

"Hell, yes."

"Okay."

"Good night, buddy."

"Good night."

They slept with their arms around one another.

✻

The two Marines were given packs and a set of black pajamas such as were worn by the Viet Cong. They started wearing the black pajamas and kept their uniforms in the packs. The knife always stayed hidden on Dodson's person. In a matter of a short time, they settled down into the routine of the prison camp, a narrow existence, where they kept to themselves, separate from the South Vietnamese prisoners. On the surface, they cooperated with the routine of exercises and the three meals a day. The food was always rice, spiced from time to time with vegetables and chili peppers. They realized that it was no accident to have been brought to this particular camp, and the more they talked about it at night, the more they began to fear that perhaps what the South Vietnamese had said was probably true. Eventually, they would be sent somewhere else where they could be useful to the Viet Cong. The intention of their captors was clearly to keep them alive and healthy. Conditions were not ideal, but they were not unbearable. Once a week, they were taken under guard to a nearby stream where they could wash themselves and their black pajamas.

Then the routine was broken; the day came when the two Marines became the center of attention. The prison hut was cleared of all the South Vietnamese except for the one who spoke English.

The Viet Cong whom Dodson called the Chief came into the room. He carried a radio and a bunch of newspapers and magazines. They were of obvious importance to him because he set them down carefully. The radio worked on transistor batteries, and he started whirling the dial until he found the place he wanted. He gave a pleasant smile as an English voice, a woman's, came into the prison hut. Dodson remembered the voice because he had heard it in Da Nang. It was Hanoi Hannah, talking sweet and syrupy and playing some very good records.

Baby love all you do is treat me bad and leave me sad — the words came out of the radio. The Supremes.

Sitting on the pounded earth floor, they listened, the Chief watching them and at the same time picking at his ear with an ivory toothpick.

"This is a square one," said Dodson, moving his shoulders in time to the music, snapping his fingers.

The Chief turned to the Vietnamese and obviously asked what had been said. The South Vietnamese had not understood, and he asked Dodson what he had said.

"Cool music."

"I still don't understand," said the South Vietnamese. "Please no tricks. This is important."

"The music is good. Real American. Hippy."

"What is hippy?"

"The latest. Modern." Dodson snapped his fingers for emphasis.

"Ah, yes, I understand. Thank you."

"Anytime."

And the South Vietnamese, beaming, translated what had been said to the Chief. With a frown, the Chief resumed his ear-picking in earnest.

The radio kept on, Hanoi Hannah promising her audience that while they were wading through the swamps, their girl friends back home were cruising around. She laughed and said, "Honey, come on now. Wouldn't you like to be home in bed, with her? Your bed out here is empty and wet. And she's found someone else. And if she hasn't now, she will when they send you back in a coffin. So here's a song to cheer you up. A sexy one."

And it was Pearl Bailey, "Ca C'est L'Amour."

It was a half-hour program. The two American Marines listened and slapped their thighs in time to the music. The two Vietnamese watched, incredulous, one a leader from the National Liberation Front, the other acting as interpreter now but in actuality a prisoner from the Army of the Republic of Vietnam. The guard standing at the door looked in on the scene, made no motion, and outdoors the sun was sinking beneath the mountains and the cold night wind wafted into the room.

Dodson and Eckes did not jump to any conclusions. They were happy to hear Hanoi Hannah. She had the best record collection in Vietnam, and whenever she spoke, they didn't listen. They were too impatient for the next record. The sound they heard was the sound of their own country, and if it worked on them at all, it wasn't in any subtle political way. It brought home to them. It gave them a lift. Then the program was over, and the Chief turned the radio off.

"Fantastic," said Eckes. "That broad is really groovy."

Again the Chief wanted to know what they had said, and after repeated exchanges to make sure the interpreter understood, it was relayed to the Chief. He looked puzzled and he said something in Vietnamese to the interpreter.

"The officer wants to know what you two think of what the lady said. He wants to know your political opinions."

"I don't vote. Don't have political opinions," said Eckes, "but she sure has musical taste."

"That's a roj," said Dodson. It took them a while to explain to the interpreter that a roj was a roger, meaning a definite, a yes, an amen.

The interpreter said that the Chief wanted to know whether they had any questions about the program, not about the music, but the other things.

"Yes," Dodson said.

"What?" said the interpreter anxiously.

"I want to know if she's American. I mean her accent is something I can't place. But she could pass."

"Yeah," said Eckes, "New York society maybe."

"What about it?" said Dodson. "Ask the Chief."

The question was relayed to the Chief, and he looked very irritated. He talked to the interpreter, and when they were finished, the interpreter said, "He is unhappy with your question. He wants to know if you think about revolution and counterrevolution."

Dodson and Eckes looked at one another with a kind of mock concern, and it was not missed by the Chief.

His voice was sharp and rapid, and he stood up. The guard at the door looked angrily at the two Americans.

"He says that he is disappointed in you. He is leaving these papers and journals with you because they contain important passages in English and he thinks you should study them. He will be back tomorrow."

For a moment the two Americans were left alone.

"Jesus," said Eckes.

"Brainwashing," said Dodson.

"That's it," said Eckes. "I read you clear when you said square one."

"They'll try to break us down, buddy."

"I know."

"They won't."

"You bet your sweet ass they won't."

They looked at each other like conspirators. At last, it had begun. This was the deadpan beginning, and it soothed them both to know that it had.

Inevitably, the day centered on the arrival of the Chief. It happened every afternoon, with the same ritual of the prison hut cleared except for the four of them and the guard at the door. It became the event by which they calculated another day having passed. At night, they whispered to one another how it had gone, and usually it was Dodson who made the assessment on how well they were holding up against the Chief. The Chief, as Dodson noted, was waiting for one of them to break. Strangely, the half hour with the Chief brought them happiness because of the music.

✿

"Dodson." It was the interpreter speaking.

"Yes."

"Today, there will be no listening to the radio. The officer wants to talk to Eckes alone. You will leave."

Dodson took his time rising. He looked down at Eckes, the young Marine who was his old friend now, and he said, "Do your best."

"Yes, sir." said Eckes.

That night, they were especially close and Eckes whispered what had happened.

"He wanted to know military stuff," said Eckes.

"You tell him anything?"

"Nothing."

"How'd he take it?"

"He just kept asking. What kind of radios? What frequencies?"

"What did you say?"

"Name, rank, serial number routine."

"He buy it?"

"That's all he heard."

"Good man."

"You'd reamed me if I'd done different. Right?"

"I suppose."

＊

"Why are you fighting the Viet Cong?"

It was the first question Dodson was asked the next afternoon. Eckes was outside now, out of sight, and he was alone with the Chief and the interpreter, and the guard lingering at the door.

Dodson looked curiously at the Chief. He was plucking at a group of long hairs on his chin. He wasn't pulling them, just feeling them. His eyes were small and black. His eyes had no lashes, and the few strands of hair over his lip were a long absurd-looking idea of a mustache.

"What does he mean?" said Dodson.

"What have you against the Viet Cong?"

"I belong in the Marine Corps. They sent me here. I follow orders."

Next there was a furtive exchange between the Chief and the interpreter.

"He says he likes you."

"Me?"

"Yes, you. Because you are a Negro."

"What's my being a Negro got to do with it? I'm a Marine Corps sergeant."

"He says that you say this because you have been misguided. They exploit your people. They keep you as slaves. You are a mercenary. You should not be fighting against the National Liberation Front."

"I'm absolutely sure of what I am and what I'm doing."

Then the conversation stopped for interpretation.

The Chief had apparently congratulated the interpreter on something he had said, and this seemed to please him.

"Do you dream of being a free man?" said the interpreter.

"I am," answered Dodson.

"He says you lie," said the interpreter, not pausing for translation. "Freedom is what the Viet Cong dream and fight for. They need it to be men as much as your race needs it in America. He says that you are not honest and that if you will listen to what he has to offer, they will give you freedom and equality in the Viet Cong and he says they are honest, not like the Americans, who are two-faced and who hate black men like you."

"How come you can go on straight like that without asking him what he wants to say?" challenged Dodson.

"He has already told me what he wants me to tell you. I say his words, not mine. He wants to give you a special case."

"Yeah?"

"Yes."

Dodson glanced at the Chief who seemed to be following the conversation, intently, as if he understood every word.

"You on their side?" said Dodson.

The interpreter turned to the Chief, speaking in Vietnamese, and then the two talked seriously for a few minutes, back and forth, and the interpreter brought his attention back to Dodson.

"He thinks we have talked enough for today. Let me say that you have done nothing to show you are an intelligent, sensitive man. My role is not as you think. I am not a traitor. I live in this land, and I find myself here with these people who are of my own blood and my own land, and well, I want to live. Now have you found them unkind? Have they beat you?"

"No."

"Have you considered that life is different in this land? It is, as he says, for the Vietnamese people, a struggle to find themselves. He says that you, a Negro, you have done nothing but defeat your own people by staying in this country fighting. He says that you should join them. He says many Frenchmen joined our brothers in the North when they saw how unfair and unjust was the fact that Vietnamese men were oppressed by the whites."

"I am a Marine."

"No, you are a Negro. You are betraying your own people and your own family by fighting against the Viet Cong. Don't you see that?"

The question was thrown at Dodson, and it burst upon him as hard as if they had struck him. They left and he sat there, staring out through the open door, where he could see the guard bringing back Eckes, and beyond, the shaded mountains with their free air.

✻

That night when they got into their sleeping positions, Dodson wasn't nearly as close to Eckes as he had been. The reason was that Dodson realized that he was afraid.

"Jim?"

"Yeah?"

"Jim? Why are you staying so far away? I'll have to shout my fucking head off to talk."

"Okay?" said Dodson. They were close now.

"Yeah? What's wrong?"

"What do you want to talk for?"

"Well, it's what we do."

"I'd like to sleep."

"You're the one who always wants to talk."

"I don't tonight."

"Okay, then let's sleep."

"Yeah."

"They try to break you down?"

"Naw. They can't."

"That's right. We're Marines."

"Yeah. Now cut out the crap."

"I got an idea."

"What?"

"I'd like to get us something, a mirror."

"I don't get it."

Eckes' hand reached out and touched Dodson's wrist. His fingers began to play out a signal, the SOS in Morse code.

"Got it," said Dodson.

The gesture on his wrist touched Dodson in more ways than the obvious. It was a signal to himself. He knew he was scared, and to his dismay, he recognized that the Chief had cut through a lot of things, talking about black and white. He lay there in the darkness with Eckes next to him, lying with his body against his.

There was something different that night. Dodson sensed that if the Chief worked on him long enough, he would break. And that disturbed Dodson. It made him feel like a pauper for the first time in his Marine Corps life that he could even imagine himself renouncing the Corps, America, his wife and his son. He came face to face with it that night. And he hated them for being able to do it through his black skin. He had never realized himself so vulnerable. The Chief could make him feel the presence of that larger thing, his blackness, against everything else that he had tried to be, a man, a husband, a father, an American. But he recognized that it was there. They could break him, if they worked at him long enough. It grieved him that it was possible, and he had the courage to admit the possibility.

Everything he wanted was out there on the other side of the mountains. But he knew there was a secret place in himself that they could claim, and it was not his desire to have them find and exploit it. It was like every part of himself, something that belonged to him, and if ever anyone was going to wrestle with it, he could do it best. If he could get back. And take Eckes with him — because that was part of going back. He was glad he had the knife.

*

One night when they were having their supper of rice, all in the same house — prisoners, guards, and the two Marines — all beneath the same thatched roof, the Vietnamese like one family, and the Marines in a corner by themselves, Eckes knew his chance had come. One of the Viet Cong guards was cutting another guard's hair. What fascinated Eckes was the mirror one Viet Cong was holding. He saw the mirror and almost immediately he knew he had to have it. For the moment he ate his rice, watching the procedure. The guard acting as barber laughed when his customer pointed to a place that was not quite right. The scissors cut as demanded and the mirror confirmed that it was done to satisfaction. Then they were finished. The barber-guard put the scissors and the mirror into a khaki canvas kit. Each item belonged in the kit and no one seemed to own it. Eckes' heart pounded as he waited to see if anyone would claim it. No. It remained there on the table against the wall along with the tin plates that were part of the camp's accepted equipment. Eckes rubbed the stubble on his chin that was really a beard now. He was rather proud of it, and he regretted what he must do, shave it off, and thus lose the age it gave him. He knew that he must cast off the beard if he wanted the mirror, and he did. He was beside himself at the thought of possessing the mirror. He was a signalman and he had discovered this talent in the Marine Corps. His contribution to the Corps was sending and receiving messages. He did nothing that night, but for the next few days, he complained that he would like to shave. And often as he spoke of it, he made it a joke. He would miss his beard.

The night that he casually walked over and claimed the kit no one noticed. He went down to the stream and shaved, and when he returned there was considerable comment and laughter. Eckes looked in misery.

His face gleamed, and he quietly returned the barber's kit to its accustomed place. The hammering in his heart didn't show, and he let the Vietnamese soldiers and the Viet Cong guards enjoy themselves and get their kicks remarking how he looked like a girl. Inside himself, he shivered, feeling the coldness of the mirror against his skin. He had already decided that if they missed it immediately, he would say that it had not been there, that he had shaved by using the stream as a mirror. In this latter regard, he had deliberately nicked himself in a few places, not bloody enough to attract attention when he came back, but there for them to see, if they had their doubts.

Eckes told Dodson that night, whispering it so softly that he felt he was mouthing every letter. Hearing it, Dodson simply nodded. The two men locked arms and said nothing more. They didn't say it, but they knew the time was near.

*

It came on the day when they figured they had been prisoners for thirty days. By this time, they were dressed every day in the black pajamas just like any other Viet Cong, and at first glance, they could have been mistaken for just another person living in the back hills where there were no Americans. They had both lost weight, and since shaving himself, Eckes looked like a choir boy more than a prisoner.

*

The Marines were told to pack. They were not told where they were going, but they were definitely leaving the camp and would not return. Three Viet Cong guards escorted them. One led the way, then Dodson and Eckes tied together, then the two guards bringing up the rear. They set a good fast pace, but there was no running, nor the long rope attached to the guards. Dodson saw this aspect as a good one. They passed through the jungle and Dodson wondered if they were taking them off to kill them. Or if they were marching them into North Vietnam, just as the South Vietnamese had suggested. There was something odd about it because the prison camp had been perfectly secure, from the Viet Cong point of view. He did not know what to believe. On a ridgeline he heard artillery firing, and he was sure it was Marine guns. They were heading North, toward Da Nang. He became conscious that first night that the guards were unusually relaxed. They were all armed with American carbines, and suddenly it hit Dodson that this was the time. He shivered with the expectation. He didn't want them to notice, but his mind now concentrated on their habits with the rifles. They had the guns. Dodson had the knife. His wrists were not as tightly bound as the guards imagined. He had used the wrist trick, and there was a tiny space of air. He had something to work on. If he could get the guns, he and Eckes could escape. Dodson that night whispered to Eckes that the time was near. He wanted Eckes to be alert. They shook hands in silent agreement.

✻

The next day, they still maintained a northerly direction. The artillery sounded louder and closer. It was something big going on. Hour by hour, Dodson watched. He noted that the guards carried their carbines carelessly. They even had the safety catches on. He could tell from the way they carried the carbines over their shoulders that they were lulled into believing that escape was not possible for the prisoners. He felt that gave *him* an advantage. They would be surprised, and he would not. He knew something they did not know. He kept working on his wrists. It made Dodson more confident. They speeded up the pace and he guessed that they must have a place in mind for the break that night. After dark they stopped and built a fire and started boiling the rice. They were sitting in a little opening in the forest, the trees overhanging the fire.

The muffled roar of the artillery continued, reminding Dodson that Da Nang was near, and that by tomorrow night, they might leave it behind. The Viet Cong were cheerful, rubbing their hands in anticipation of the meal.

Dodson watched the three men put their carbines up against a tree. He saw this out of the corner of his eyes, and he didn't want to turn and stare. His wrists were loose, and he carefully got the knife out of his waist and cut his hands free. He had committed himself. This was the time. The tension increased in him. He was gambling that the guards would leave the carbines up against the tree when they sat down to eat. He didn't tell Eckes what he was thinking because he would jinx his chances. He got ready when he saw the three Viet Cong leave the carbines there. They joined him and Eckes at the fire. They had their tin dishes out, ready to eat the rice.

The carbines were ten feet away, unattended, and everything in Dodson was now alert. He waited until the three Viet Cong had the rice in their dishes, waited excruciatingly, until they were settled down, and then he was ready.

He placed his plate of rice down on the ground before him, quietly, nothing abrupt, putting it down with tenderness, precision, and a studied carelessness as if he were an artist putting on the last dab of color to a painting he had worked on for years. Then bracing himself, he sprang up.

He made two mighty jumps. The Viet Cong shouted, but Dodson was at the tree. He grabbed a carbine and cocked it. He whirled and let out a bloodcurdling yell.

The three Viet Cong were open-mouthed. At the yell they dropped their dishes and they ran.

For a moment, Dodson stared unbelieving and his hands shaking; then he said, "Let's move fast."

They lost no time. Dodson threw one of the carbines to Eckes. He grabbed the third and the packs the Viet Cong had left behind. They started running, going back up the mountain. They went into the jungle, avoiding the trail. They ran all that night. They reached the top of the mountain, and started down the other side in the direction that Dodson felt was north. The artillery had stopped, and he cursed its silence because it would have given him direction. The run was exhausting, and the density of the jungle fatiguing, but they kept running. They did not talk except for once when Eckes said, "That yell you gave. It made my hair stand on end. Where did you ever learn that?"

"It just came out that way," said Dodson.

When first light arrived, they paused to examine the contents of the packs. They were getting heavy and they decided to lighten them. The packs were loaded with rice. The Marines also found a package of hard candy and a canteen filled with water. They decided to keep their own packs with the Marine fatigue uniforms which they would need when they got close to their own lines. For the present, they decided to continue wearing black pajamas. They abandoned the third rifle, reasoning that it was in the way and additional weight. They also left the rice and took the candy and the water.

They didn't think of sleep. They were too exhilarated in the knowledge that they had gotten away, but despite this, they knew that the real test was in getting back to Da Nang. So they kept going, the jungle never changing, always thick, always stifling, always dark, and it abused them mightily.

They didn't joke about having made it. They were too cautious to talk about that, or about anything, and there was considerable weight on them that if they talked now, if they dreamed now, it would all disappear. They felt they could keep going for days and nights.

They had no idea how far it was to Da Nang, only that it lay to the north and that was their goal. By the second night, their path had taken them back up to a mountain top and Dodson began to sense defeat. It looked remarkably like the same mountain of the first night, and, bitterly, he surmised that they had traveled in a circle. Instead of getting farther away from the Viet Cong, they had come back dangerously close to the prison camp. Discussing their dilemma, still talking out of long habit in whispers, they were startled to hear rustling in the bush. Abruptly, sickeningly, they knew they were not alone. Cover. They burrowed down into the elephant grass. They lay very still. They heard their hearts pounding and it was the unhappiest sound of their experience. They clutched their carbines and they felt the sweat in their hands alive with their fear. The rustles came nearer and they distinguished the sound of footsteps, cruelly close, taunting them. The Viet Cong were moving cautiously, obviously looking for them. The Viet Cong signaled to one another with whistles and the sound of them so near was a stress, a stress to remain immobile, a stress not to jump up and run. Lying there they realized how much they wanted freedom and their mouths became dry as the searchers beat all around them. They lay with their faces down, their bodies rigid, not looking at one another, not breathing when three Viet Cong passed within two feet of them. They were surprised when they were not found. The Viet Cong footsteps went farther away, the sound of the grass sliding against black pajamas faded and the grip of panic that lay on them faded, too. They stayed there through the entire night, never moving, never thinking that they should get up because every time they thought of moving, a shiver of fear hit them. All night, tense, trembling, wary, they waited. Their pajamas were soaked in sweat and their bodies were cold. They endured in silence and gratitude that the black night protected them.

Suddenly night was over. Without a word they knew it was time to get up. In a crouch, they moved swiftly down the mountain. They found a stream that headed north. The stream became their guide. Where it went, they followed. Occasionally they looked backwards, grateful that the mountain was now clearly behind them; after another day, the pattern of the stream began to widen. They seized on this as a hopeful sign. It could be a branch of the main river that flowed down through Da Nang and emptied into the China Sea.

❀

Often, bone-weary, they lay on the ground, exhausted, panting, and once when this happened, they heard a distant sound of pounding. It became louder, deafening, and they looked up and saw a herd of water buffaloes crashing toward them. It was an earthquake of sound and they ran, not daring to look back, the stampeding sound clapping down on their senses. They climbed into a tree with the herd perhaps eighty yards behind them. From their perch, they looked down and saw the thunderous herd pass beneath them.

"We got to keep going," said Dodson.

Eckes agreed.

❀

Twice they saw light American planes, and Eckes used his mirror to send out a signal. But the planes never saw them.

They stuck to their plan of staying with the river, but one afternoon, walking along the banks, their senses were again jolted. They felt themselves suddenly sinking into the sand. The shock was unbelievable. They began to scream, breaking their silence. They were being sucked into the vicious slime, and in a terrified determination, they pulled their way out.

"Christ," said Eckes, "quicksand?"

"Whatever it was, it wasn't good," said Dodson.

From then on, they picked their way carefully and avoided anything that in any way resembled the slime of that ground.

They kept following the stream that had now grown into a respectable river and on the fourth night of their flight, they saw a light on the horizon. When they saw it, they hardly expected it. Round and round it went and they took a deep breath, and together they said, "Da Nang."

"It's got to be a searchlight at the airbase," said Dodson.

To make sure, they climbed to high ground. Each step up had a new kind of suspense because they knew that if it were Da Nang they were nearly home. They weren't saying it yet. They waited until they got up there and from ahigh they saw their goal. It was Da Nang, and the emotion of seeing the lights of the base swept over them. They looked at each other.

"Buddy," said Eckes, "I think we've made it."

"We've made it," said Dodson.

Otherwise they were quiet. They took off their black pajamas and they put on their Marine Corps fatigues and they started walking toward the lights.

＊

Two days later, in Da Nang, I saw them, in new uniforms, and they were not gauche or immodest, two brave men who told their story, and in New York City, when my film report was edited for presentation on the Huntley-Brinkley Report one of the editors called up Eckes' mother to ask her what she thought of her son. She stammered in speechless disbelief, and then said the first thing that came to her mind, "But my boy never got into any trouble before."

In York, Pennsylvania, when Dodson's wife got the news she began to cry. She picked up her baby, and holding him in her arms, she joyfully thanked God for her husband's life. Then she put the baby back in his crib and she sat down to write Dodson her daily letter.

And the war went on.

THE FACE OF SOUTH VIETNAM

PART II

photographs by Jill Krementz

layout by Robert Conrad

photographs printed by
George Martin and
Igor Bakht

For Ira Rosenberg
J.K.

.LONG LIVE THE SPIRIT OF MUTUAL ASSISTANCE OF THE PEOPLES AND GOVERNMENTS OF THE FREE WORLD NATIONS
.MUTUAL AID MEANS MUTUAL SECURITY
.THE VIETNAMESE PEOPLE ARE GRATEFUL FOR THE ASSISTANCE OF FRIENDLY COUNTRIES
.EVERY MEASURE OF ASSISTANCE IS A NEW STEP TOWARDS THE TRIUMPH OF FREEDOM OVER SLAVERY

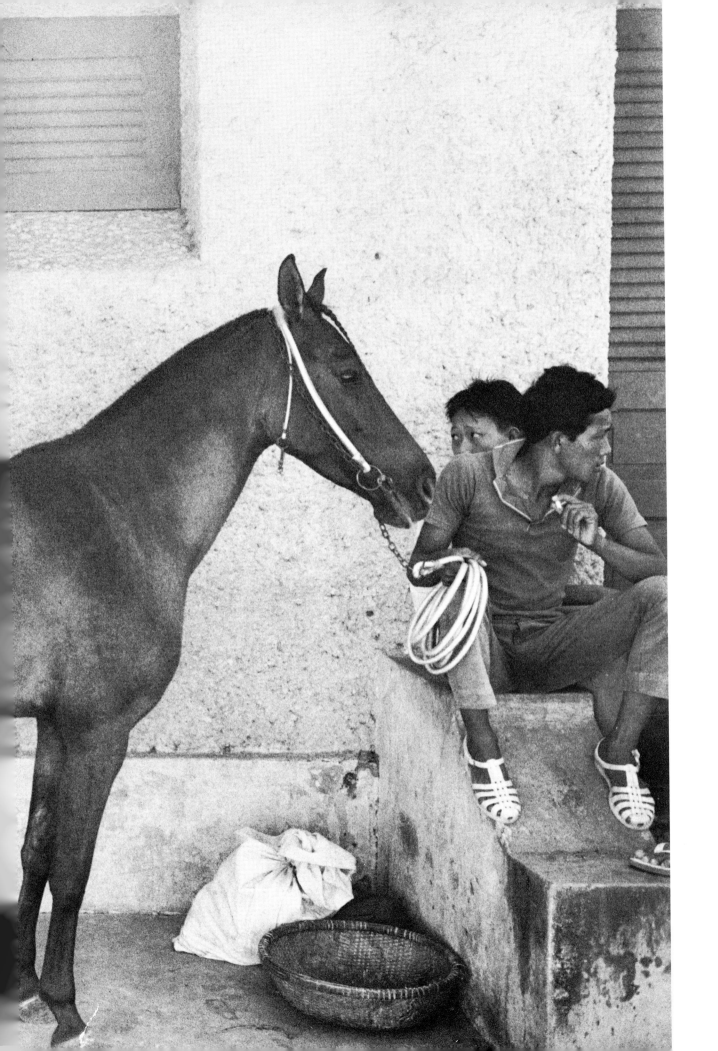

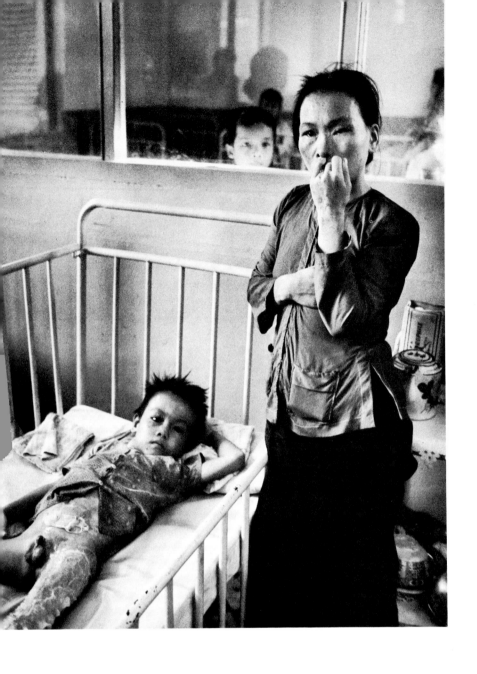

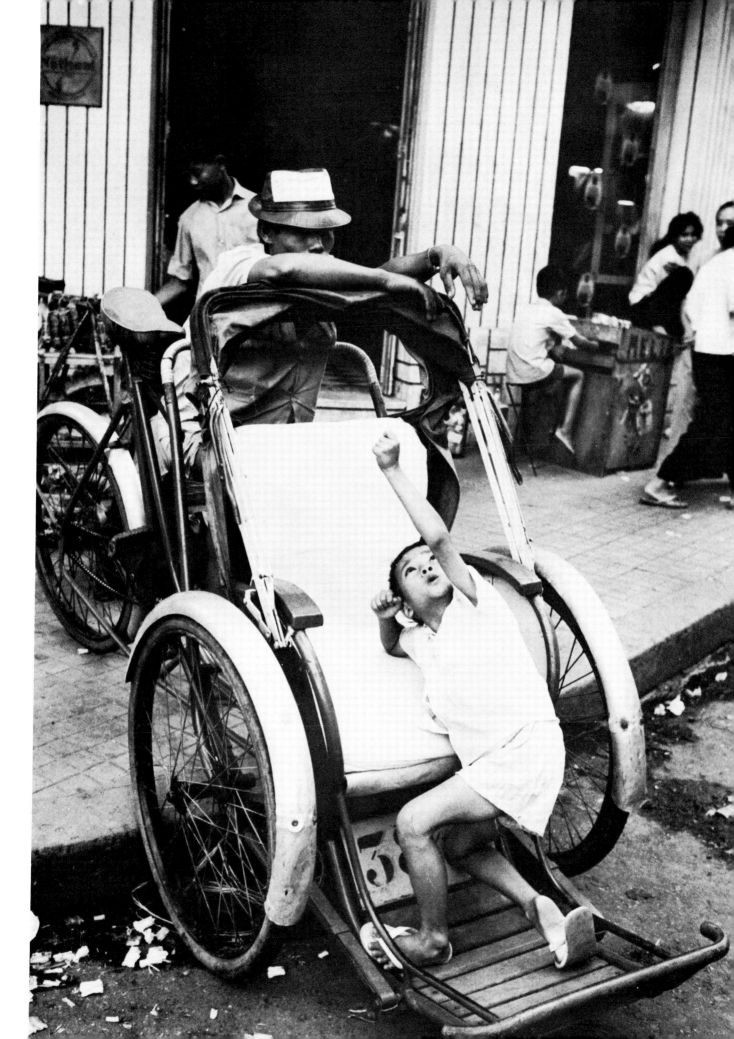

191

LIONS D'AFRIQUE PHIM MÀU PHỤ ĐỀ VIỆT NGỮ
萬獸之王
非洲探險原始野獸实地拍攝大彩鉅片

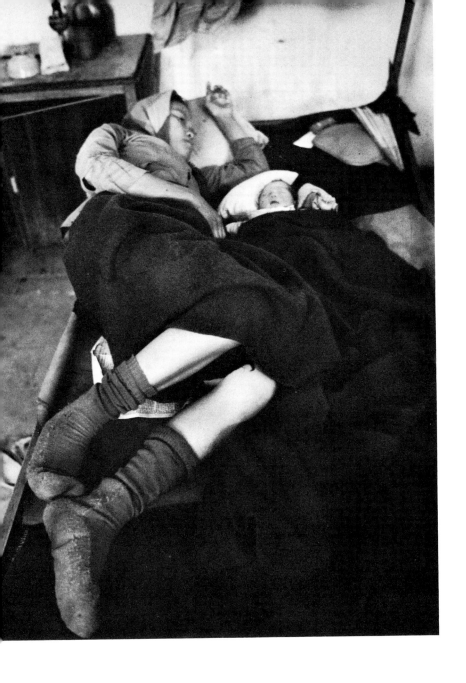

212

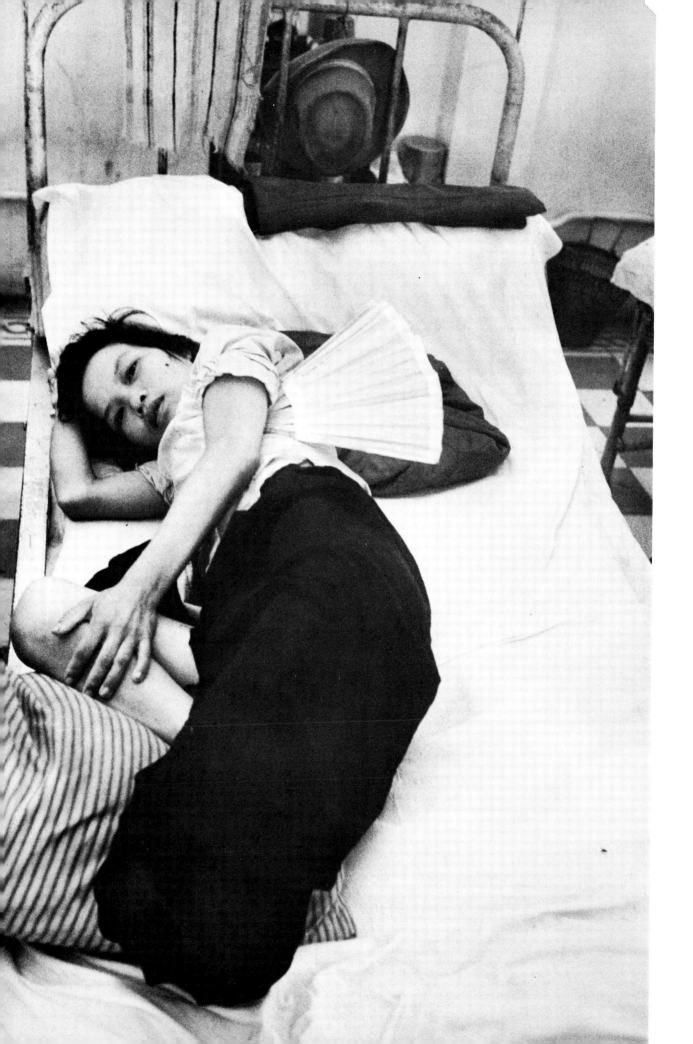

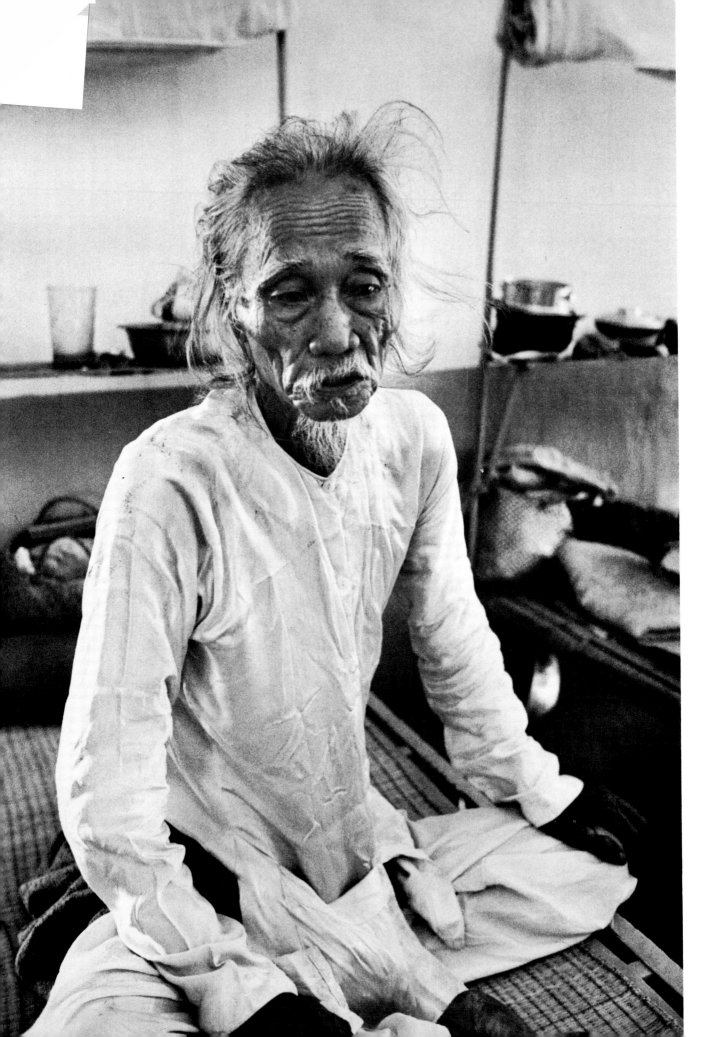

231

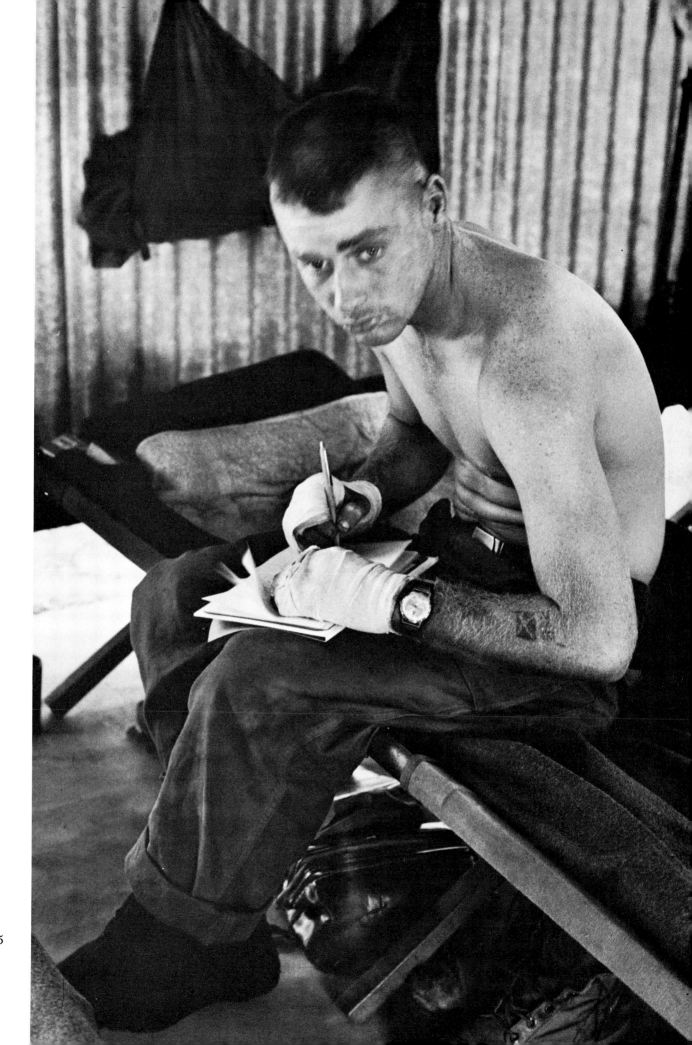

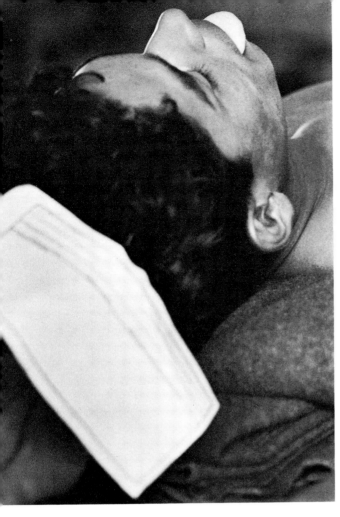

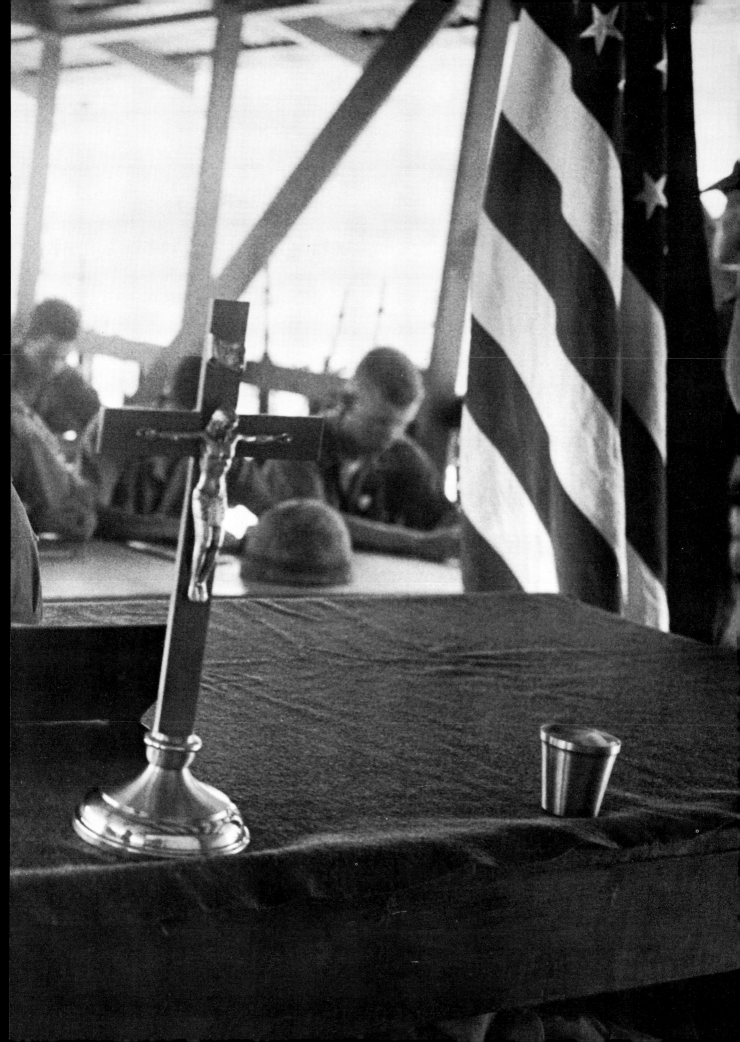

ABOUT THE PHOTOGRAPHS

Page 115. April 14, 1966. Saigon: A Vietnamese anti-riot soldier on duty at a demonstration against Premier Ky's government. He stands in front of a medical poster. The demonstration convened in the afternoon outside the Buddhist Youth headquarters. By evening the air was heavy with tear gas and an American jeep had been burned.

Page 116. April 1, 1966. Saigon: Vietnamese children swimming in a small pool that is in the center of a traffic circle in downtown Saigon. Earlier that morning the Victoria Hotel, an American servicemen's billet one mile away, had been bombed.

Page 117. December 6, 1965. Saigon: United States Ambassador Henry Cabot Lodge at the *Cercle Sportif*, a private club owned by the French. The Ambassador went there for a swim practically every day around lunchtime. This is the only place in Saigon where Americans can go to swim and play tennis in safety.

Pages 118–119. January 15, 1966. Saigon: Tan Son Nhut Airport. General Westmoreland (3rd from left), Vietnamese Foreign Affairs Minister Tran Van Do (4th from left), Ambassador Henry Cabot Lodge (hand on chin) and others are waiting for Secretary of State Dean Rusk and Ambassador W. Averell Harriman.

Page 120. January 15, 1966. Saigon: Tan Son Nhut Airport. The plane lands.

Page 121, *top*. October 23, 1965. Saigon: Tan Son Nhut Airport. *Center,* Senators Edward M. Kennedy and Joseph Tydings hold a press conference upon their arrival in the V.I.P. Lounge. Senator Kennedy came primarily to look into the refugee situation.

Page 121, *bottom*. January 15, 1966. Saigon: Tan Son Nhut Airport. Ambassador Lodge, Secretary of State Rusk and Ambassador Harriman.

Page 122. May 17, 1966. Saigon: A small store near the entrance to Tan Son Nhut Airport. Hand-tinted photographs of President Johnson and President Kennedy are a common sight in Saigon.

Page 123. April 10, 1966. Easter Sunday, Saigon: Vien Hoa Dao. Buddhist boy scouts hang a picture of Buddha on a wall prior to a press conference held by Thich Tri Quang.

Pages 124–125. April 12, 1966. Saigon: Premier Nguyen Cao Ky's house at Tan Son Nhut Airport. The Prime Minister's daughter peeks in while her father (in a short-sleeved shirt) demonstrates his new television set to American newsmen, (*left to right*) Dean Brelis of NBC, Ward Just of the Washington *Post* and Emmet Hughes of *Newsweek*. Ky gave a small dinner for the newsmen which was held outdoors with everyone seated at a long table. Behind the Prime Minister, on the lawn, was his private helicopter, and while we ate we could watch his deer grazing only a few feet away. "Aloha" was embroidered on the pocket of the Prime Minister's shirt, and I remarked that he must have done some shopping in Honolulu — he had just returned from the conference there with President Johnson. He replied that the shirt had cost him eight dollars and that this high price had discouraged him from any further shopping.

Pages 126–127. April 12, 1966. Saigon: Premier Ky's living room.

Page 128. May 24, 1966. Saigon: National Armed Forces and People's Congress. Ambassador Henry Cabot Lodge listens to a translation of Premier Ky's opening speech. The Congress was discussing the forthcoming elections and the need for a constitution.

Page 129. January 15, 1966. Saigon: Premier Ky.

Pages 130–131. October 28, 1965. Saigon: The changing of the guard at Gia Long Palace, the Vietnamese chief of state's office. This is where the 1963 anti-Diem coup took place.

Pages 132–135. May 10, 1966. Saigon: I was awakened at 6:00 A.M. by the sound of gunfire. From my window at the Hotel Caravelle I could see the intermittent gun flares. I quickly dressed and went downstairs. The Suzy Wong Tailor Shop on a nearby street had been blown up and American MP's on duty in the area had spotted a truck which was immediately suspect, since it was the only vehicle in sight and was moving away from the scene of the explosion. (The truck had, in fact, nothing to do with the explosion. It was subsequently found to contain a number of Vietnamese men, women and children on their way to work at the waterfront.) The MP's fired on the truck and when the truck did not stop, continued to fire. Other MP's on duty at the opposite end of the street immediately assumed that there was a VC attack and, seeing the truck advancing toward them, opened fire on it. The first group of MP's then thought that they were receiving hostile fire from the truck. What ensued was a fire fight between American MP's, with the truck carrying the Vietnamese civilians caught in the middle. The firing continued for twenty-five minutes. Five Vietnamese were killed and twenty-six wounded. Eight Americans were also wounded. That afternoon at the five o'clock briefing it was announced by the American spokesman that the families of the dead and wounded Vietnamese would be paid compensation by the American government. The picture on pages 132 and 133 shows the suspects who were held for questioning but released within an hour. On page 135 — an abandoned bicycle which may have carried the bomb that blew up the tailor shop.

Page 136. April 4, 1966. Saigon: The bus is common transportation around the country.

Non-Vietnamese are discouraged from using buses because of the likelihood of Communist ambush.

Page 137. May 1, 1966. Hue: Thich Tri Quang, the impassioned bonze who, in 1966, led the unsuccessful Buddhist struggle against the Saigon military regime.

Page 138. May 21, 1966. Saigon: Vien Hoa Dao — monks on a hunger strike protesting against the Ky government. At the far left is a Buddhist novice.

Page 139. March 2, 1966. My Tho: Third Field Hospital — a Vietnamese soldier who lost his arm. The hospital was so crowded that even the outside corridors were filled with beds. Still, there were many civilian hospitals where patients often had to lie on straw mats on the floor because there were no beds.

Page 140. July 14, 1966. Can Tho: Province hospital in the Mekong Delta, 80 miles south of Saigon. About 500 civilians enter this hospital each month and of these cases, about 300 require major medical surgery. The hospital was built in 1895 by the French Colonial administration and was the first civilian hospital in the Delta. It has 456 beds and is the only hospital available to the estimated total of 420,000 inhabitants of its province. There are about 12 amputee cases a week, some of which are double amputations of both arms and legs, for many civilians are wounded by land mines and booby traps.

Page 141. January 31, 1966. Bien Loi (near Saigon): An orphanage.

Pages 142–143. March 6, 1966. Saigon: Sunday afternoon at Phu Tho, the race track in Saigon. The track is swept by a mine detector beforehand. Ten to fifteen thousand people attend the track on an average Sunday. The admission is eight cents. Both horses and jockeys are strikingly small by Western standards — a good horse may be twelve hands high and a jockey may weigh sixty-five pounds. Horse racing is the favorite sport of the Vietnamese.

Page 144. December 1, 1965. Saigon street scene.

Page 145. August 24, 1965. Saigon: Art Gallery. Many of the local artists are strongly influenced by Modigliani.

Page 146. January 31, 1966. Bien Loi: Vietnamese houses often consist of only one room in which as many as a dozen members of the family may live.

Page 147. January 14, 1966. Cholon: Saigon's twin city and home of half a million Chinese. The Chinese businessmen control at least 70% of the economy of South Vietnam.

Page 148. March 2, 1966. My Tho: At a civilian hospital, I went into a ward filled only with cribs. In each crib lay a child, severely burned. A mother or an older sister or brother stood beside each crib. Some maintained an unmoving vigil; others continuously fanned away flies. The children themselves lay silent; they were in too much pain even to cry.

Page 149. September 1, 1966. Saigon: This child is pretending to shoot down an American airplane.

Pages 150–151. January 22, 1966. Da Nang: Some Vietnamese children whom I had met on a previous visit took me to this exhibit of captured Vietcong weapons, which was set up in the center of the city. Martial music blared out of the loudspeakers. The weapons were mostly Chinese.

Page 152, *top and bottom*. March 31, 1966. Saigon: A Buddhist demonstration against the Ky government. The Vietnamese carried anti-American signs.

Page 153. March 31, 1966. Saigon: Demonstrators attach a notice denouncing Prime Minister Ky to the base of a statue of a Buddhist girl killed in the first Buddhist demonstrations against President Diem. They have a song commemorating her which they sing at most demonstrations.

Page 154. February 25, 1966 (Trung Sisters Holiday). Vung Tau: Girl students taking part in the day's festivities. They carry a sign which says "Eliminate the Vietcong in order to be in the nation." The holiday is primarily for women.

Page 155. May 19, 1966. Chuong Thien Province: A reception committee for Premier Ky who flew down for the day. He opened up a new road, visited a refugee center, admired some new pigs and, after lunch at the province general's house, was presented with two fighting cocks.

Page 156. March 2, 1966. My Tho in the Mekong Delta: Four schoolgirls.

Page 157. December 3, 1965. Saigon: A Vietnamese girl.

Pages 158–159. April 10, 1966. Saigon: Vien Hoa Dao Pagoda. While Thich Tri Quang held a press conference inside one of the main buildings, these Buddhist girls were playing ring-a-round-a-rosy outside. The girls dance and sing every Sunday afternoon.

Page 160. April 10, 1966. Same as pages 158–159. Vien Hoa Dao: Blindman's buff.

Page 161. May 21, 1966. Saigon. Vien Hoa Dao: Buddhist nuns on a hunger strike. They sat for hours in the hot sun.

Page 162. January 14, 1966. Cholon: A street vendor's wares.

Pages 162–163. May 11, 1966. Near Saigon: A Buddhist altar in a small village.

Pages 164–165. May 4, 1966. Hue. Tu Dam Pagoda: The statue at the altar is of Thich Quang Duc, the first Buddhist monk to commit suicide by burning himself to death with gasoline.

Pages 166–175. April 14, 1966. Near Saigon: A Vietnamese funeral. *Page 166:* Three women kneeling in front of the coffin prior to the burial. *Page 167:* A musician at the cemetery. *Pages 168–169:* At the grave. Relatives in high mourning wear roughly made robes of gauzy cotton. Men wear headpieces of coarsely twined straw and women wear veils. The remaining kin in low mourning wear white bands neatly wound around the head. The son of the deceased carries a roughly cut cane and he is required to lean upon it, bending low, during the procession when the coffin is borne by the pallbearers to the grave site. The photograph of the deceased and various objects and offerings which have been brought along on a portable altar will be carried home and placed on the family altar. *Page 170:* The eldest son holding burning joss. *Page 171:* Mourners at the cemetery. *Page 172:* The photograph of the deceased on the ancestral altar in his house. Visitors are expected to bring gifts of food, cash or alcohol. *Page 173:* The widow prostrate before the altar. *Pages 174–175:* Mourners returning from the funeral.

Page 176. February 4, 1966. Bien Loi near Saigon: Black pajamas, the traditional peasant costume, drying in the sun.

Page 177. May 2, 1966. Hue: The Imperial Palace.

Pages 178–179. March 31, 1966. Saigon: The public execution place in the Central Market. At an anti-government demonstration, Buddhists placed crude likenesses of President Ky and General Co on the execution stakes. Minutes after this photograph was taken, Vietnamese security police ripped them down.

Page 180. May 11, 1966. Saigon: A cabinet in the living room of a middle-class Vietnamese family. The snapshots on the left are of members of the family. On the right panel, on the bottom row, third from left, is a picture of Thich Quang Duc immolating himself. Many Vietnamese families have this picture hung in a prominent place in their houses. I had gone there for a wedding of a friend. The groom's father had been executed by Madame Nhu.

Page 181. April 18, 1966. Phan Rang: A VC decoy used for target practice in the 101st Airborne's training program.

Page 182. May 19, 1966. An Xuyen Province. Premier Ky negotiating a muddy path. Following him is Province Chief General Quang, who was later dismissed.

Pages 182–183. February 25, 1966. Vung Tau: A section of the fifty-nine-man reconstruction teams trained at the Revolutionary Development Cadre Training School in Vung Tau, a resort town 45 miles southeast of Saigon. The teams, all of whose members wear the black Vietcong-style pajamas, are armed but rely on military backing from the government troops in the area.

Pages 184–185. July 16, 1966. Pleiku: Truong Son Cadre Training School for the Montagnards. The Montagnards are primitive hill people of South Vietnam, whom the Buddhists traditionally abhor because of their lack of so-called culture. They do not vote and are therefore not subject to military conscription. However, they must often protect themselves from the VC.

Page 186. April 19, 1966. Phan Rang: GI's armed with PX-purchased cameras zero in on a USO performer.

Page 187. The performer.

Pages 188–189. April 18, 1966. Phan Rang: The Royale Bar, one of the many bars along what is known as "The Strip." The portrait hanging on the wall is that of The Madame ("Mamasan"). I had spent the entire afternoon at the Royale because someone had told me that Tuesday was the day the girls received their weekly penicillin shots. While the girls received a great deal of attention, none of it seemed to be medical and I returned to the base camp for dinner. When I arrived in the mess hall, a number of majors invited me to sit at the colonel's table. They asked me where I had been photographing that afternoon, and when I told them I had gone to the Strip to watch the girls get their shots they appeared to be totally unaware that such a routine existed. I went on to explain that I hadn't gotten any pictures, and they appeared very relieved. I then mentioned that the reason I hadn't gotten any pictures was because the shots had evidently been discontinued. Majors are usually self-assured. This group had been. They weren't any more.

Pages 190–191. February 27, 1966. Vung Tau: A pilot's room.

Page 192. February 27, 1966. Vung Tau: A pilot's pinups.

Page 193, *top.* January 20, 1965. Saigon: A sign on the wall in the Public Information Office at Tan Son Nhut Airport. *Bottom:* April 17, 1966. Phan Rang Airport.

Pages 194–199. May 11, 1966. Near Saigon: At the wedding of my friend Hanh, a Vietnamese hairdresser. *Page 194, top:* Hanh presents the groom to her eighty-six-year-old grandmother. *Page 194, bottom:* Pinning a flower on the groom. *Page 195:* The cake. *Pages 196–197:* The ceremony. *Page 198:* The bride and groom on their way to a reception at the groom's house. *Page 199:* The reception. It is traditional for the older women to converge on the hardwood bed in the center of the main room where they gossip and chew betel.

Page 200. April 30, 1966. Hue: A fortune-teller's sign.

Page 201. January 14, 1966. Cholon: A Chinese movie poster.

Page 202. November 11, 1966. Saigon: Dolls are a favorite GI souvenir.

Page 203. February 25, 1966. Vung Tau: The end of the South Vietnamese peninsula.

Pages 204–209. May 16–17, 1966. Refugees moving from Ban Thach to Cam Ranh Bay.

Page 210. April 25, 1966. Da Nang: Old women fishing for shrimp.

Page 211, *top.* June 28, 1966. Kontum: A seventy-three-year-old Montagnard father with his two sons. He told me that his thirty-five-year-old wife was working in the fields. *Bottom:* April 5, 1966. Da Nang: Interior of a peasant's house.

Page 212. June 28, 1966. Kontum Province Hospital (Maternity Ward): GI socks.

Page 213. June 22, 1966. Qui Nhon Province Hospital: What I remember most about this hospital is that a corpse lay on the floor in one of the main wards, covered with flies.

Page 214. March 2, 1966. My Tho Province Hospital: An old man wounded in a skirmish between GI's and the Vietcong.

Page 215. December 9, 1965. Near Saigon: An orphanage.

Page 216. February 22, 1966. Bien Loi near Saigon: Barbed wire left by the French.

Page 217. April 9, 1966. Saigon: Three hairdressers. My friend Hanh is in the center.

Pages 218–219. April 18, 1966. Phan Rang (Base camp of the 101st Airborne): Crapshooting at an N.C.O. Club.

250

Page 220, *top.* April 26, 1966. Da Nang (Company B, 3rd Tank Bn., 3rd Marine Division): GI's returning from the shower. *Bottom:* February 26, 1966. Vung Tau: GI's on R & R.

Page 221, *top.* January 23, 1966. Da Nang: Before going out on evening patrol. *Bottom:* January 11, 1966. Bien Hoa: Jo Ann Collins, who flew over to deliver an issue of *Playboy* in keeping with the magazine's policy that anyone who orders a lifetime subscription is entitled to have the first issue delivered by a playmate of his choice.

Page 222. February 26, 1966. Vung Tau: An Australian soldier on leave. He cherishes a collection of seventy-three tattooes.

Page 223. April 19, 1966. Phan Rang: Mashed potatoes.

Pages 224–225. January 25, 1966. Da Nang: After a mortar attack at the airbase.

Pages 226–227. June 23, 1966. Pleime: There are well over two thousand U.S. helicopters in the air above Vietnam.

Page 228, *top.* April 19, 1966. Phan Rang. *Bottom:* June 24, 1966. Between Dong Tre and An Khe: An air strike against a village in the Central Highlands.

Page 229. April 29, 1966. Da Nang: Few Green Berets survived the desperate battle of Ashau. *Top:* At attention as the band plays "Fearless Men Who Jump and Die." *Bottom:* Here Purple Hearts are being distributed.

Pages 230–231. June 22, 1966. Qui Nhon. Thompson Beach: The sign on the right reads:

THOMPSON BEACH
U.S. ARMY SUPPORT
QUI NHON
Dedicated to the memory of
Pfc. Troy M. Thompson, Jr.,

71st Transportation Co. (Terminal Service),
who lost his life in the service of
his country on 26 September 1965.

Page 232. May 25, 1966. Tan Son Nhut Airport: Between planes.

Page 233, *top.* February 13, 1966. Tan Son Nhut Airport: Following a visit from Vice-President Humphrey. *Bottom:* May 16, 1966. At sea: After delivering the baby of a Vietnamese refugee aboard the U.S.S. *Page.* The baby was named "Page."

Page 234, *top.* July 12, 1966. First Division Headquarters: Tagging captured Vietcong weapons. *Bottom:* April 24, 1966 Da Nang: Booby Trap School.

Page 235. April 17, 1966. Phan Thiet (D Company of the 326th Medical Battalion, 1st Brigade/ 101st Airborne): Letter home.

Pages 236–237. April 18, 1966. Phan Rang: 101st Airborne paratroopers are briefed for their first combat patrol in Vietnam.

Pages 238–239. June 24, 1966. An Khe (Base camp of the First Cavalry): An operation begins. The orders — sweep and destroy.

Page 240. November 29, 1965. Saigon: Third Field Hospital. The fatigues and boots of GI's who have been killed or wounded are stored in Conex cases in back of the hospital.

Page 241, *top left and right.* April 17, 1966. Phan Thiet Aid Station: Casualties. *Bottom:* June 24, 1966. An Khe Second Surgical Hospital: Notations of shrapnel removed from wounded GI's.

Pages 242–243. April 24, 1966. Da Nang: Memorial service for a dead Marine.

Page 244. June 22, 1966. Qui Nhon: The U.S. Army's permanent installation for receiving those who die in Vietnam.